W9-DDA-109

HOW TO GROW YOUR OWN TOBACCO

HOW TO GROW YOUR OWN TOBACCO

FROM SEED TO SMOKE

★ RAY FRENCH ★

Cool
Springs
Press
Growing Successful Gardeners™
www.coolspringspress.com
Brentwood, Tennessee

First published in 2011 by Cool Springs Press, an imprint of the Quayside Publishing Group, 400 First Avenue North, Suite 300, Minneapolis, MN 55401 USA

Certain sidebars were adapted from sources other than the author. Please see page 152 for a listing of them.

Library of Congress Cataloging-in-Publication Data

French, Ray, 1968-
How to grow your own tobacco : from seed to smoke / Ray French.
p. cm.
Includes index.
ISBN 1-59186-488-7 (alk. paper)
1. Tobacco. I. Title.
SB273.F74 2011
633.7'1--dc23

2011021245

Editor: Billie Brownell
Illustrations by Mark Ross, Surfaceworks Design Studio

Photos by author and Shutterstock.com, except: Alamy, p. 11 (Kurt Moebus/imagebroker), p. 37 (Vespasian), p. 83 (Matt Meadows/Peter Arnold, Inc.); iStockphoto.com, p. 29, 51 top; Courtesy of CTGR/University of Tennessee, p. 48, 49, 51 bottom; Courtesy of The Tobacco Seed Company, p. 55, 57, 59.

Printed in the United States of America

10 9 8 7 6 5 4 3 2 1

DEDICATION AND ACKNOWLEDGMENTS

I dedicate this book to my wife, Ginny, who has supported my pursuit of a career in the plant world and all of my endeavors. She does not smoke, but she did help take care of my plants in the garden when I traveled. What would I do without her?

I would like to thank Cool Springs Press for their encouragement with this project. I would like to thank my family, who put up with me on nights and weekends as I sat in the glow of our computer in between trips or after working in my office all day. Finally, I would like to thank my friends, who tried and enjoyed growing their own tobacco.

ill.1 Seed leaflets emerging

ill2. First "true" leaf emerges - Time to transplant to pots from the seed tray

ill3. Time to transplant to gard

ill.4 Garden layout

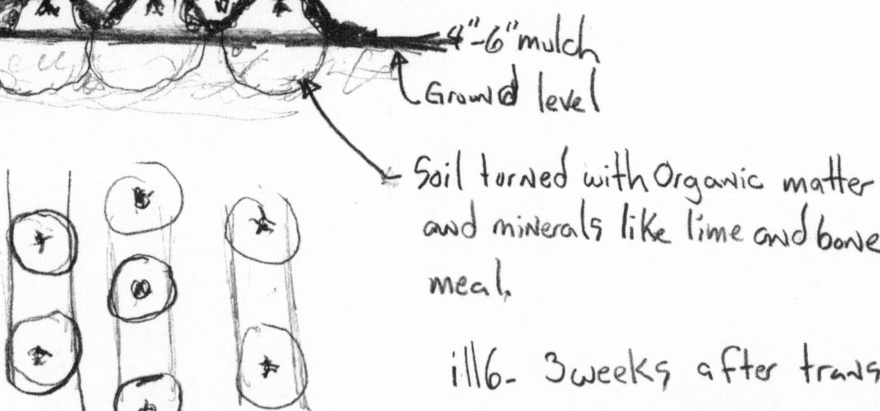

ill5 - Alternate spacing on rows

ill6- 3weeks after transpla

CONTENTS

INTRODUCTION

ONE OF THE COMPELLING REASONS I WROTE THIS BOOK WAS TO TALK ABOUT ORGANIC TOBACCO GROWING. I AM PASSIONATE ABOUT NOT KILLING OUR SOILS AND PROMOTING SUSTAINABLE AGRICULTURE; I HAVE SEEN FIRSTHAND THE EFFECTS OF PESTICIDE EXPOSURE. FROM STUDYING ORGANIC CHEMISTRY AT AUBURN UNIVERSITY TO HOLDING A LARGE-SCALE COMMERCIAL PESTICIDE LICENSE FOR MANY YEARS, I CAN TELL YOU THERE ARE CLASSES OF CHEMICALS THAT REALLY ARE DANGEROUS TO BE AROUND (MUCH LESS SMOKE).

So, armed with that knowledge and the experience of managing large-scale commercial horticulture operations, and having owned and run my own organic produce farm, I have learned first-hand that it is possible to control bugs by raising healthy plants and occasionally using soap and oil sprays. With a little time and attention you really can have clean, healthy, and better tasting plants. My motivation in writing this book is to teach people that organic growing and sustainable gardening really are easy, and they do make a difference.

I hope that as a result of experimenting with growing tobacco you'll learn how fun and easy it also is to garden. There are so many amazing and cool things that you can do with plants. Once you get the hang of it, plant plenty of flowers to brighten up your garden and home and be sure to plant food for you and your neighbors' tables.

I have a story to share: I have a painting on the wall of my office that was given to me by the Duggar side of my family, and dedicated to me with a plaque inscribed with the words "Keeping up the Tradition." This painting commemorates the one-hundredth anniversary of the Auburn University Old Rotation Farm Experiment. My great-uncle John Frederick Duggar started this experiment while he was a professor of Agronomy at Auburn—and the same plot is still farmed using his techniques today. John Frederick Duggar went on to write many editions of his popular textbook and eventually he became the Dean of Agriculture. The painting commemorates

the farm crops that have been used in this rotation for more than 110 years now: wheat, vetch, oats, corn, rye, cowpeas, soybeans, crimson clover, and cotton. This farm is still one of the most fertile pieces of farmland in the state of Alabama. The very same farming practices my great-uncle demonstrated in 1896 still apply today, and yet very few farmers follow these simple crop rotations. Many modern farmers depend on the use of chemical fertilizers and pesticides instead of being conservation minded. As a result, much of the farmland in the United States is depleted of nutrients and is being sustained by

the use of chemical fertilizers, pesticides, and genetically engineered crops. Each year we become more and more dependent on these practices. With deforestation and urban sprawl also taking their toll we need to start taking care of our farmland for future generations.

My decision to write this book was not taken lightly in view of the health risks associated with smoking. But I have often wondered why cancer and breathing disorders are so prevalent in modern times yet, as I learned researching this book, humans have used tobacco since the time of Mayan civilization. Maybe it's not the tobacco itself that is causing disease, but all the stuff added to it. Who knows for sure? But by growing and curing your own tobacco, and using the methods I describe in this book, you can be sure you're using the plant in its purest form, without the man-made chemical additives and pesticides.

How did it turn out? Well, I loved growing tobacco in my backyard, and I truly enjoyed ordering the seed, planting the seed, growing the plants, curing the harvest, and sharing it. It was a positive experience hearing the stories and memories people have about the plant from their childhood. It is also a great dinner party novelty to pull out a bag of tobacco you grew and see the reaction your guests have when they start rolling and smoking their own cigars or cigarettes. After receiving a resounding thumbs-up, I confirmed my suspicions that my homegrown organic tobacco really was nice and well worth the effort.

GETTING STARTED

1

WHY SHOULD YOU GROW YOUR OWN TOBACCO? THE REASONS RANGE FROM AVOIDING WHAT BIG TOBACCO MAY HAVE ADDED, TO AVOIDING TAXES, TO SAVING MONEY, OR JUST FOR ENJOYING THE SATISFACTION OF SMOKING SOMETHING YOU HAVE GROWN YOURSELF. THE LAST ONE IS A PRETTY GOOD REASON. THE ENERGY OF DOING SOMETHING NEW, THE PRIDE OF DOING SOMETHING WELL, AND THE ENJOYMENT OF YOUR HARVEST ARE ALL GREAT REASONS TO GROW YOUR OWN.

Thinking about writing this book caused me to ask myself several specific questions that you may have on your mind too:

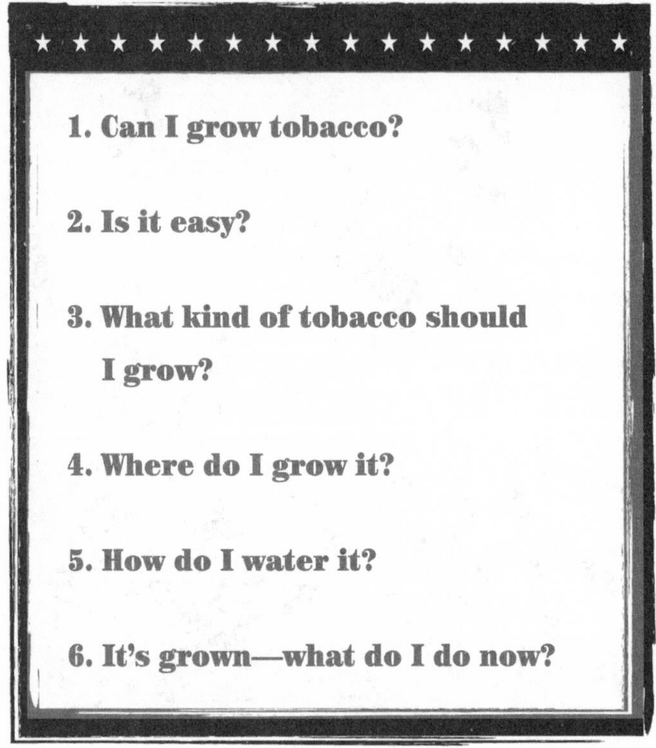

1. Can I grow tobacco?
2. Is it easy?
3. What kind of tobacco should I grow?
4. Where do I grow it?
5. How do I water it?
6. It's grown—what do I do now?

This book is dedicated to answering all of these questions. So if you decide to grow tobacco, I hope you will have as much fun with it as I did, and that you will be glad you did it. Then you will be planning next year's crop as you are enjoying this season's harvest.

You can grow tobacco plants in containers on your deck, in your backyard garden, or use them as ornamentals in your front yard flowerbeds. I have heard from so many people how fun and easy tobacco can be to grow. I know you can do it.

The Economics of Growing Your Own Tobacco

"Sin taxes" have made the smoking or chewing of tobacco products so much more expensive than it has ever been before. Recently, I saw a pack of cigarettes priced at $14.50 in New York, and cigarettes were selling for $15 a pack in Australia. Most modern cigarettes also have many chemical additives, from ones to make cigarettes burn more slowly in order for the manufacturer to use less tobacco, to the new chemicals recently added to make cigarettes self-extinguish when they are not being smoked. It's pretty shocking; but most brands of cigarettes are known to be full of additives.

There have also been many accusations leveled against manufacturers claiming that additives to increase the inherently addictive nature of tobacco and cigarettes are added to some of the most popular brands. And listen to this—completely separate from anything a manufacturer may add is yet another consideration: most farmers spray dangerous chemical pesticides on tobacco plants to kill bugs. While there are some companies that do sell natural cigarettes, I have seldom seen true organically grown tobacco sold in the market. However, I really do not want to dwell on what commercial tobacco does or does not have in it. I would like to propose that there is a certain flavor, pride, and enjoyment that comes from growing your own tobacco.

We All Know the Risks

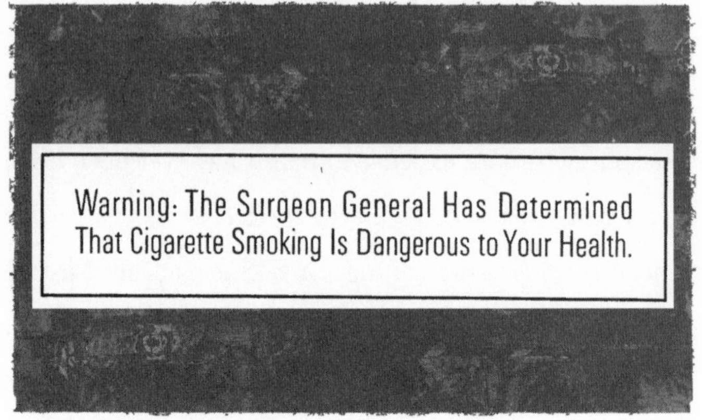

Warning: The Surgeon General Has Determined
That Cigarette Smoking Is Dangerous to Your Health.

The science says that tobacco is bad for your health.

Whether you roll it and smoke it, chew it and spit it, snort it, or put it in a pipe, tobacco is harmful to your body—especially when used in excess. Yet there are millions of people who use tobacco every day and they have no idea where it came from or what is in it.

The purpose of this book is not to introduce new people to tobacco, but to offer a homegrown alternative. The satisfaction of growing and curing your own tobacco and of being the first one in your neighborhood to grow tobacco is great fun.

Why growing your own is a good thing.

I've talked about that certain satisfaction and pride that comes from growing, harvesting, and enjoying something you have made and processed yourself. By preparing a home-cooked meal, the experience is often exponentially better than eating frozen dinners or going to a fast food restaurant—it becomes a tangible product you can be proud of having made yourself.

If you have already consciously decided you want to use tobacco, why not grow it yourself using the healthiest possible methods? This book covers organic production techniques that can apply to other plants as well, from flowers to peppers to tomatoes and whatever you may be growing in your garden that makes you happy. The techniques I describe will make you a better grower, and if you enjoy the process and your goal

Tobacco Tidbits

- The snorting of snuff became popular in the eighteenth century.
- Philip Morris was established in the United States in 1847.
- RJ Reynolds was founded in 1875.
- Cigars became the rage in the nineteenth century.
- Between 1900 and 1950 cigarettes were popularized. The Duke family controlled the cigarette market by controlling the patent on the cigarette machine. They soon became some of the wealthiest people in the world.
- The Camel brand was introduced in 1913.
- The movie *Superman* had the first big product placement where, for a $40,000 placement fee, Lois Lane smoked for the first time on camera. In addition, Superman's battle scenes were against backdrops of cigarette ads.
- Until recently cigarettes were given to soldiers as part of their daily rations.

is personal satisfaction, then the results will be much more rewarding. You should give it a try. In the end, the satisfaction of enjoying a season in the garden and having something you are proud to have made will give you immense pleasure.

Experience Not Required

Growing organically and sustainably does not mean you have to join the counterculture—you don't have to let your hair grow long, stop bathing, or even play drums all night. Sustainable agriculture and organic growing is an approach that starts a chain reaction of ridding your garden shed, closet, yard, and life of the nerve agents, chemical fertilizers, and pesticides that are worse for you than the tobacco. It also makes for healthier plants and a long-term approach to gardening that will produce amazing results year after year. These practices won't destroy the earth and are actually typically easier and less expensive to use. Many modern large-scale farmers have become dependent on chemicals and that type of farming and are not able or willing to make the switch to sustainable agriculture. Some growers have learned how to grow commercially without all these harmful pesticides, and I have seen time and time again that they not only found organic techniques easier but more profitable in the long run. It means getting in the habit of being a good grower.

Who, me, be a good grower? Yes, you can be a good grower. Just follow a few easy steps outlined here.

★ ★ ★ ★ ★ ★ ★ ★ ★ ★ ★ ★ ★ ★ ★ ★

How To Be A Good Tobacco Grower

1. Plant on time.
2. Create great soil.
3. Develop good watering habits.
4. Prepare for your climate.
5. Mix in plenty of sunshine and some tender loving care.

These are all part of the formula for success.

This all sounds too easy, right? Well, arming yourself with the basic information covered in this book and developing some great growing habits will make it easier no matter what your level of experience is.

A happy gardener makes for a great garden. If you take the approach of growing tobacco as a fun pastime or hobby then you will be sure to have an amazing garden. This could be a hobby that leads to a lifetime of enjoyment and pleasure. Think about comparing notes with your friends and enjoying the fruits of your labor. Start a garden community and bring many friends into the loop. Share a few seeds and a few laughs about ways to torture and kill aphids. Smoke it up while sharing a common interest.

But, if you approach growing your own tobacco as a chore and a means to an end then you will struggle for sure. A happy gardener will spend more time checking on plants. This is the best thing anyone can do. There is an old adage that the best fertilizer is your own footprint. This is so true. Physically being in the garden will allow you to see if bugs are eating your plants, if they are too wet, if they need harvesting, or if they need fertilizing. These things are all easy to recognize, but you must show up to notice them. Build a routine around checking out your plants. Spend some time with them.

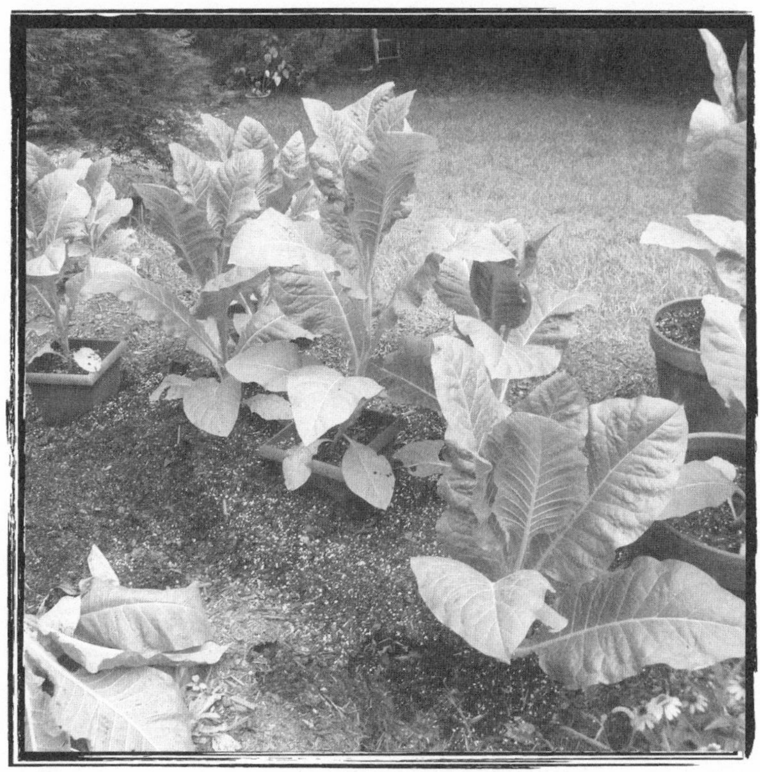

I encourage you to develop a community garden approach like so many home-brewing clubs and garden clubs have done. Compare tobacco grades and varieties you like with other people in your area or on Internet forums and websites. Share different curing and fermenting techniques. As a member of the International Plant Propagators Society, I have long taken their approach to sharing information about growing. Their motto is "Seek and Share," so seek out formation and freely share it with your fellow gardeners whether it is tobacco, vegetables, or whatever you enjoy growing, and you will more often than not learn something of value in return.

Is It Legal?
How Much Can I Expect From One Plant?

In most areas of the world it is not illegal to grow tobacco for your home use. It is illegal in the United States, however, to barter or sell tobacco leaf that has been processed unless you have a permit. The FDA has the authority to regulate tobacco products for sale but that does not extend to the growing of tobacco or the use of it by an individual who has grown and processed it for their own consumption.

You don't have to grow many plants to have enough tobacco to last several years. *One plant* can yield as many as 100 cigarettes over 4 to 5 pickings. Twenty-five pounds of cured tobacco leaf should yield 1,000 cigars, allowing for the wrappers, binders, and fillers. You will not need a huge number of plants to supply what you can consume in a year.

Tobacco keeps extremely well so long as it is dry and free of insect infestations. Cigar makers store it for at least a year compressed in bales covered in burlap. Some of the cigarette tobacco sold today in modern cigarettes may even be as much as 10 years old. You don't have to keep it that long, but if you do decide to plant a larger plot then it does store well. Many aficionados believe that tobacco ages like a fine wine, and it's especially true of cigar tobaccos.

Tobacco has a very interesting history that is entwined in our modern lives and in the history and stories from the ancient Indians of the Americas. Tobacco is what drove the English to send ships to trade with the American colonies. It has had both social stigmas and social standing. It has paid for governments and built great universities. It has been both loved and hated all around the world. Let's find out why.

THE HISTORY OF TOBACCO

2

TOBACCO GREW NATURALLY IN THE WILD ALTHOUGH THERE IS EVIDENCE OF ITS CULTIVATION DATING TO 6,000 B.C. THE MAYANS SPREAD ITS USE AS FAR NORTH AS THE MISSISSIPPI VALLEY BETWEEN 470 AND 630 A.D. NATIVE AMERICANS MIXED TOBACCO WITH OTHER AROMATIC HERBS AND SMOKED IT AS CRUDE CIGARS. THE ARAWAK INDIANS PRESENTED CHRISTOPHER COLUMBUS WITH TOBACCO WHEN HE ARRIVED ON HIS FIRST TRIP FROM EUROPE.

Tobacco is a plant of tropical origin, and it is a perennial, not an annual. This is an important distinction in that we treat it as an annual because we harvest its leaves (not its flowers, fruits, or seeds); in fact, flowers should be removed when they appear.

Native Americans grew and smoked tobacco, and the use of tobacco was and still is an important part of their cultural traditions. It was revered and smoked on special occasions and during ceremonies, and was also reported to have been chewed, consumed in a tea, smeared on their bodies as a paste, and even used as an enema! They were quite creative.

Tobacco became a social status symbol and was even used as currency. It was a form of payment in the colonies for a wife; the price was 125 pounds of tobacco (about a bale) for a woman who had made the voyage from Europe to Virginia to be a

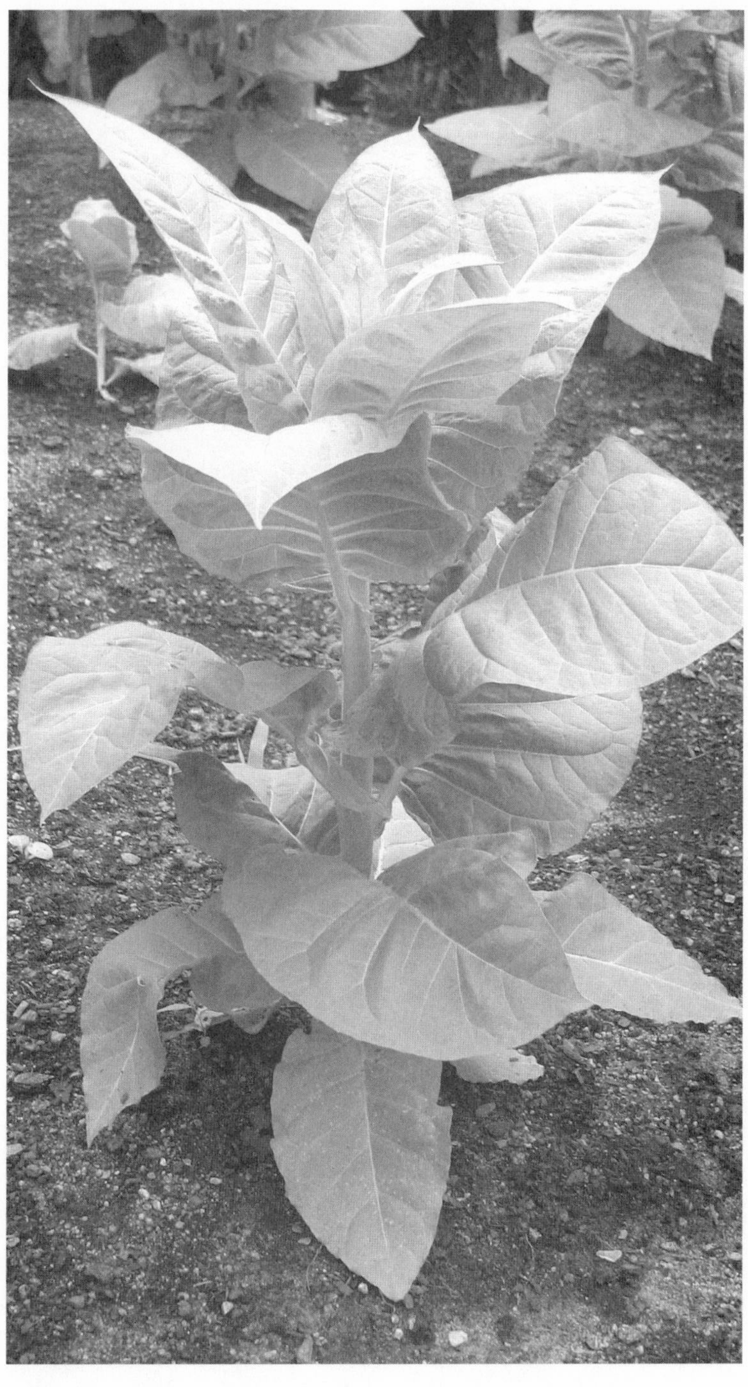

The Victorian Introduction of the Cigarette

In an attempt to civilize anything that seemed coarse or uncivil, much of Victorian society would adapt cultural items to suit their tastes. This human manipulation of tobacco included chopping it up, wrapping it in a man-made piece of paper, and then inserting it into a piece of cane for a mouth piece. This was just another way of civilizing part of the coarser aspects of the British Empire. A feministic culture dominated smoking at this time and this gave further rise to the "dainty" cigarette, bearing a feminine name.

★ ★ ★ ★ ★ ★ ★ ★ ★ ★ ★

bride. Soon after also began the history of governmental control and the taxation of tobacco to the point that governments in the Western world became dependent on money garnered from tobacco taxes. (They still are to this day.)

The Europeans touted the healing and medicinal properties of tobacco. It was used in wraps and poultices to heal sprained ankles. It has also been been ground up and mixed with water as a spray to kill insects. By the end of the sixteenth century, the first reports surfaced from the medical community of the negative health effects and addictive properties of this prized plant.

The Commercial Allotment

Until recent times, tobacco was the most profitable crop a farmer could legally grow.

Historically, farmers were required to have an allotment from the United States federal government in order to grow tobacco. This was determined by the amount of tobacco your family grew prior to 1955, and you could lease or sell your allotment to growers in other areas or on your farm. This protectionist program allowed a few families to become very wealthy and made tobacco one of the most profitable farm crops an American farmer could grow legally. The federal tobacco program ended in 2003, meaning anyone can now grow tobacco, although the growing of tobacco is not nearly as lucrative as it once was. (You must still apply for a license to *process* tobacco under current law, however.)

Tobacco Growing Regions

Tobacco was traditionally grown in the United States on the East Coast and in the South. New England, Long Island, Virginia, West Virginia, North Carolina, South Carolina, Tennessee, Kentucky, Georgia, parts of Alabama and Mississippi, and

Tobacco Tidbit

Following a tobacco-industry recession, (1680–1720), production grew rapidly and by 1740 the Chesapeake Bay region was exporting 50% of the combined production of the world's tobacco-raising regions. The increase in production, however, was not due to better farming methods, but a result of increasing human slavery and the clearing of virgin land. Chesapeake planters imported over 100,000 Africans between 1700 and 1770.

Louisiana outside New Orleans were the most prominent locations. Some tobacco allotments were eventually leased to some Midwest growers as well. Tobacco has been grown outside the United States and all around the world. Any part of the world that gets at least 75 frost-free days can grow tobacco. The richest soils grow the best plants; farmers typically have avoided planting tobacco in bad spots.

Tobacco has been grown, harvested, and cured in several very different ways. It's been grown both in the full sun and under shade structures. It's been harvested one leaf at a time, starting from the bottom and working up the plant as the leaves matured, and also harvested as a whole plant.

The area outside of Hartford, Connecticut, has been renown for its high-quality, shade-grown tobacco since the early 1900s. These are considered the finest grade of leaves. They are used primarily for cigar wrappers. The growers constructed shade structures that covered and enclosed the crops in a cheesecloth-type fabric. It not only protected the leaves from insects and sunburn, but it made the leaves grow larger and thinner, making

Tobacco—Born in the USA

After the American Revolution, many countries never resumed trade with the newly formed United States, but consumption of tobacco in the U.S. grew. American tobacco customs began to switch from the earlier pipe smoking to the cigar, as well as chewing tobacco, which was linked to the great American Western icon of the spittoon. The latter two were considered a more coarse form of taking tobacco and were deemed very "American" by Europeans. Americans also enjoyed the flavor of island tobacco more, but since many smokers in the USA were not wealthy, working farmers started smoking tobacco grown from their own land. This may also have come more from the American desire to be independent, not only in a legal sense by being a free-nation, but economically as well.

★ ★ ★ ★ ★ ★ ★ ★ ★ ★ ★

them better for cigar wrappers. To be a cigar wrapper, a leaf has to be perfect, with no holes, and flexible enough to hold up to the making of the cigar. The leaves lower on a plant would usually be used as filler for the inside of the cigars, and the upper leaves matured into the highest grades.

Virginia, as well as North and South Carolina, Georgia, and northern Florida, became known for their golden leaf varieties, which are used for fine-cut tobacco that is used in cigarettes and pipes. The states of Kentucky, Ohio, Tennessee, and the higher altitudes of Virginia, North Carolina, and Indiana tended to grow more of the burley types. Cuba was and is famous for their Havana varieties. As farming evolved, farmers all over the world selected the seeds for the types and plants that were best suited for their growing conditions and methods of curing. They would typically store and save their own seed. This was done by selecting the very best plants and allowing the blooms to mature into seeds, which were then harvested, dried, and stored for future seasons.

Tobacco drying in the United States was done by tying leaves in bundles and then hanging the bundles on sticks inside a tobacco barn. Growers in many areas of the United States would cure the tobacco and control moisture levels during the drying process by building a small hardwood fire that was allowed to smolder on the floor of the barn. This smoke would also flavor the leaves and season them in addition to turning them a darker color. This type of curing is mainly for pipe and chewing tobacco (burley and dark tobacco). These wooden barns were once prevalent in the tobacco growing areas but now they are beginning to disappear as modern day farmers have changed to using heated air forced through enclosed metal containers that resemble a shipping container. This method of curing is known as "flue cured." (This method of using higher heat was discovered in 1839 quite by accident. A worker in Caswell County, North Carolina, fell asleep while tending a small curing fire. The fire became quite large but instead of ruining the tobacco, it cured with a golden color, giving rise to the flue-cured style that is most prevalent today.)

The farmers in some areas would construct wooden triangles on the edges of the fields and cure the tobacco under the sun as it was harvested. This, of course, was called "sun cured." The curing and fermenting processes of tobacco were

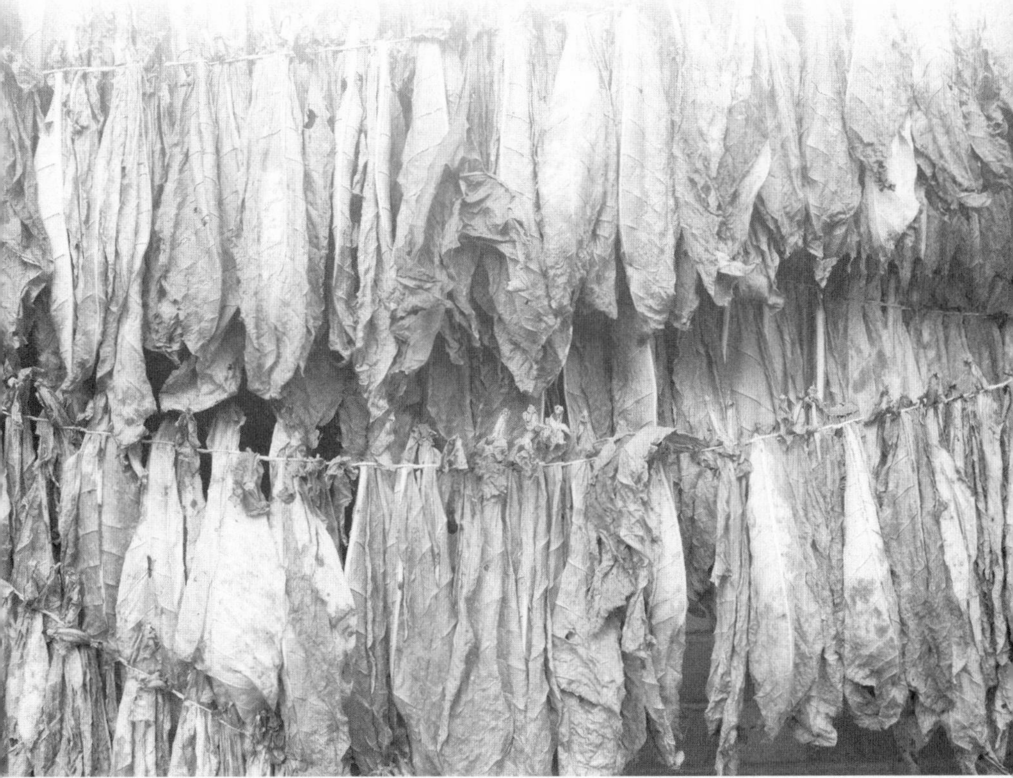

often a closely guarded family or company secret passed down through generations.

During Colonial times, the tobacco industry learned that when the leaves were stacked in tight bundles in the holds of the ships they would cure even further, actually improving the flavor. This led to the practice of aging tobacco for a mellower flavor and to improve the palate taste for the end user. The growers in Louisiana outside of New Orleans grew a thick-leaved variety known as Perique. This strongly pungent type is actually fermented under pressure for years before it is sent to market. Small amounts of the Perique tobacco would be added to cigars, pipe, and cigarette blends to give depth to the flavor. The Perique industry in Louisiana has revived somewhat. Acreage dedicated to its production has increased in the last several years, and there are several growers. They are concentrated in one parish along the Mississippi River west of New Orleans.

Just as the curing of tobacco is considered by many to be an art form, so is the blending process. The

Tobacco Tidbit

Early Native Americans in the eastern United States grew *Nicotiana rustica*, which was the first form of tobacco introduced in England and Portugal. *Nicotiana tabacam*, first introduced to the Spanish, was obtained from Mexico and South America. It has been the preferred tobacco species since settlers in Jamestown, Virginia began growing it. Because planters believed that tobacco had to be grown in virgin soil, tobacco gradually made its way farther south as the land became settled in the northern parts.

mixing and making of the blends, which give a product its particular flavor, is something that took a great deal of training and experience. The blending experts were often either the company owners or long-time trusted employees who would actually go to the market to hand-select leaves from the many different grades. Blenders combined smelling and handling the tobacco to determine exactly how it should be blended. Processors would typically purchase the tobacco dry and then do the final fermentation and flavoring themselves. In Cuba they would soak the leaves in water with a particular wine added to it. Rum and sugar were also used in the fermentation liquid by some of the processors. There are many different types of flavorings and methods that have been used over the years, some of which will be covered in the chapter on drying and curing.

Pesticides and the Tobacco Industry

With the invention of cigarette-making machines and the advent of the advertising age, cigarettes become increasingly popular around the world. Cigarette smoking in the United States hit a peak in the 1960s with an average of 6,000 per person per year smoked. Smoking has been declining in recent years, though, and is banned in many public places. There is now often a social stigma associated with being a smoker.

Cigarette advertising is limited by the government and there are many anti-smoking campaigns in place. In modern times, the government has raised taxes to discourage smoking. However, we may never see tobacco use banned outright because the government depends on the tax revenues that are generated by the sale of tobacco.

The history of commercial tobacco farming is closely tied to the growth of the pesticide industry. Some of the most harmful pesticides were invented for and used on tobacco. Tobacco itself has even been used as a pesticide. Dangerous chemical insecticides were used heavily by tobacco farmers until they were banned. The chemical methyl bromide, which is being phased out and banned, was used by farmers to sterilize the soil. Chlordane and Temik were two other favorite bug killers of old-time farmers that were so dangerous that they were also eventually banned. These chemicals may persist in the soil for decades in the areas where they were used.

These insecticides were actually often poisonous byproducts of paint and other chemical manufacturing. The pesticide corporations diluted them to the point where they would not burn (damage) plants but would still kill bugs. Unfortunately, the same insecticides that killed the bugs through the destruction of their nervous systems were also nerve agents that caused the same effects on people. Oh yeah, acetlycholinesterase

Tobacco Tidbit

Tobacco companies recommend up to 16 separate applications of pesticides just in the period between planting the seeds in greenhouses and transplanting the young plants to the field.

inhibitors stay in human bodies forever in what is called "bio-accumulation."

Gone are the days of a guy standing in the field with an umbrella to mark each pass of the crop duster as the chemicals rained down on him, but modern farming still relies heavily on some insecticides. Commercially, protective gear such as a gas mask and a Tyvek™ suit are required by law for applications of many of the same chemicals that you can buy off the shelf under different trade names, like Sevin dust. Commercial farmers still have to depend on some of these compounds to protect their crops, but you as a home gardener should not use them or even have them in your home or shed where you can breath the fumes or be exposed to them in any way.

In the last several years, the level of production in the United States has diminished for burley tobacco but held steady for flue-cured. A blow to some American tobacco farmers was the repeal of the tobacco allotment program in 2003. This event led to increased offshore production of burley and the inability of the U.S. tobacco farmers to make as much money on their tobacco crops as they once did. Flue-cured tobacco acreage has held steady despite the end of the federal program. Tobacco growers contract with companies, and while the number of individual growers has decreased, the size of farms has typically increased. Flue-cured tobacco grown in the United States is considered the best in the world, but the quality of offshore burley leaf is not that much different from the U.S.-grown burley. The reduction of the popularity of smoking in the United States and the high price of cigarettes has led to a decline in tobacco usage.

Tobacco continues to play a major role in our society and government. Indoor smoking bans are being enacted all over the world. I was in Amsterdam a few years ago on the momentous occasion of the implementation of the indoor tobacco-smoking ban there. Despite many predictions of the end of the bar and restaurant business, the smokers have just learned to adapt by smoking less and going outside.

The cheaper popular commercial cigarettes many people love so much today have an origin of convenience and have contained a typically lower grade of blended tobacco.

Cigar and fine tobacco lovers are a contingent of the tobacco users who often tend to appreciate some of the subtleties and processes of tobacco usage and making. They tend to play around with the finer types and blends and often only occasionally partake. Cigar and pipe smokers usually do not inhale, allowing the smoke to circle away while they enjoy the aroma. Cigar and pipe smokers tend to take the time to enjoy the process of slowly smoking and enjoying all the flavors possible with well-grown, processed leaves. The time they spend smoking is more of a time for reflection and deep thought; it's not as much of the hurried smoking done in a rush for a quick cigarette.

Cultures and trends have changed over the centuries and the use and production of tobacco continues to be a part of our society in many parts of the world. The art of growing and curing it was a closely guarded secret for many generations. Even to this day, the exact formulas for some of the top cigar producers are held closely.

I hope you enjoy your journey to finding the perfect formula for your climate and situation and producing your new favorite blends of tobacco.

52
52
52
M
50
50

GRADES, TYPES, AND VARIETIES OF TOBACCO

3

TOBACCO GRADES ARE BASED ON THE STALK POSITION OF THE LEAF, THE COLOR OF THE LEAF, AND OTHER PHYSICAL PROPERTIES SUCH AS LEAF THICKNESS, OIL CONTENT, FLEXIBILITY, AND SO FORTH. LEAF CHEMISTRY CHANGES WITH ITS STALK POSITION. MOST OF THE GRADING HAS TO DO WITH THE COLOR AND FLEXIBILITY OF A LEAF AFTER IT IS CURED.

There are over one hundred grades of tobacco based primarily on color and quality. Some drying methods, such as smoke curing, will produce a darker leaf, used primarily for pipe and chewing tobacco. Flue-curing produces some of the brighter colored leaves for cigarettes. Some tobacco varieties have a more golden color and there are even some with red coloration that will turn gold even before the curing process begins. Variety can and does influence the grade and use, but grade is also determined by the quality of the plant and by the method and quality of the drying and handling of the leaves after they are picked. Fermenting will also darken the leaves, producing the darker type of tobacco used in cigar fillers, pipe tobaccos, and chewing tobaccos.

In cigar-wrapper-style tobaccos, all stalk positions can be used. The best-quality leaves can be cured to wrapper grade from the bottom to the top, with some variation. The mid-quality leaves form the binder, and the lower quality leaves are the filler. Only cigar types are grown for wrappers. The leaf should have no holes and have the right color and flexibility. For burley and flue-cured, whose primary use is for cigarettes, the leaf chemistry, color, and weight typically change as the stalk position changes. Lower leaves have less nicotine content and flavor, while upper leaves are heavier, have more nicotine, and are generally more aromatic. Cigarettes and pipe tobacco are made from blends of different grades and dryness to make them burn evenly and have the right overall color.

TYPES OF TOBACCO

Burley

Burley

Burley

There are several different types of burley tobacco. These are used often in making pipe tobacco blends. As a class of tobacco, burley is the second most popular type in modern times; it's air cured, which makes it simpler to process for the home gardener. It is considered full-bodied and has a low amount of sugars. Burley burns slowly, making it particularly nice for people who enjoy the relaxing process of smoking a pipe. Burley is great to add to mixes and absorbs flavorings extremely well.

Virginia flue-cured

Virginia (or Flue-Cured)

This is one of the most popular types of tobacco. Valued for its golden hue and smooth flavor, Virginia accounts for more than 60 percent of all tobacco grown in the world today. It blends well with other types for use in cigarettes and burns nicely with a minimal amount of processing. Virginia contains a large amount of simple sugars. It is considered to be medium in overall strength in taste. It's also referred to as "bright tobacco" because of the bright gold and even orange colors it will turn when it's flue-cured.

Dark Tobacco

Dark tobacco is both a variety and a method of curing. This tobacco is a type that is typically grown in Kentucky, where they developed a specialized method of curing it. It has a very high nicotine content. This type was historically cured using smoke from hardwood fires—dark fired—but it can also be air cured similar to burley—dark air-cured. It is used as a blend, typically in small amounts, and it is very aromatic with a light flavor. Its primary commercial use is in chewing tobaccos and snuff.

Cavendish

Cavendish is an English method for curing pipe tobacco. Usually Virginia tobacco is used but sometimes burley was (and is) in the mix. In the past, farmers would take fire-cured tobacco, steam it, and then press it into blocks. It was then stored for several months to further develop the fermentation and curing. Originated by Sir Thomas Cavendish in the sixteenth century, the leaves were dipped in sugar to "mellow" the tobacco. This type of curing in modern times has become synonymous with the curing of flavored pipe tobacco. Tobacco is often mixed with rum, bourbon, cherry, vanilla, chocolate, strawberry, raspberry, mint, walnut, and even coconut flavors. In the chapter on curing, I discuss a quick-cure method similar to this that involves boiling and pressing the leaves.

)ark

)ark

Oriental Nenad Bumbić

Oriental

This is a sun-cured type grown historically in Eastern Europe. They actually cure it in the open air stacked on frames in the fields in full sun. Oriental tobacco is now grown in Turkey, Greece, and some of the other Mediterranean countries. Oriental types are used commercially in blends of exotic cigarettes. These types are often referred to as Turkish tobacco and used in mixes smoked in hookahs. (A hookah is an Asian pipe for smoking tobacco consisting of a flexible tube with a mouthpiece attached to a container of water through which smoke is drawn and cooled. A hookah is what the caterpillar character was smoking in *Alice in Wonderland*.)

Perique Courtesy of Greta's Organic Gardens

Perique

One of the most expensive, Perique tobacco is a special type that is grown in St. James Parish, Louisiana, outside New Orleans. It is a slow-burning and harsh-tasting variety. The leaves are very thick and narrow. It is typically fermented in barrels under a great deal of pressure for a year or more after the initial drying. Workers actually take it out of the oak barrels during the process and repack it to make sure it is evenly fermented. This type is great to add in small amounts to pipe and cigar blends. It should not be used on its own. I grew some in my garden and it did extremely well. It does not grow too large and makes a nice container plant.

Cuban

Cuban is world famous as a cigar type of tobacco; there are several good varieties in this class. Cuban is used in blends and mixes in pipe tobacco, as well. This type seems to be well suited for growing in hot climates.

VARIETIES OF TOBACCO

The seed companies have great descriptions of the varieties they sell in their catalogs and websites. I have profiled a few of the more popular varieties here and added some personal comments.

Virginia Gold

Virginia Gold #1

This variety performed very well in my garden. Though its seeds are extremely small, the germination rates are usually very high. I found Virginia Gold #1 to be easy to grow. This variety is usually the primary component for cigarette and pipe blends, but it is also good for cigar filler.

Virginia Dark

Virginia Dark can be used for cigarettes and in pipe blends. It is a very fast-growing type and will mature in 60 days. This one is great for beginners.

Lizard Tail Orinoco

This is a selection of Virginia tobacco from the Virginia Orinoco region that has been commonly grown over the years and is still grown today. Lizard Tail Orinoco is a tall-growing tobacco with thick, textured, crinkly leaves that are spaced closely together on the stalk. It will produce a rich brown pipe tobacco. It is a favorite of many pipe smokers, but also makes a good blending tobacco for cigars and cigarettes.

Izmir

Izmir is an Oriental type that's great for cigarette blends. It is mild and sweet with a strong, unique aroma. It can also be mixed in pipe blends.

Monte Calm Blonde

Monte Calm Blonde is a favorite European variety that has wide, thin leaves and is used for cigarettes and as cigar wrappers. It grows up to six feet tall in ideal growing conditions.

Maryland 609

This tobacco variety has a great reputation for being easy to grow and cure. Maryland 609 is a very tall variety.

Narrow Leaf Madole

Narrow Leaf Madole struggled in my garden and never really grew. It may perform better farther north. It's a dark type of tobacco widely grown in Kentucky, and it can be air- or fire-cured.

Havana (Cuban)

Havana is great for cigars, of course, and makes a superior cigar wrapper, binder, and filler. Its seeds are a little bit larger than other tobacco seeds. It may be difficult to grow and germinate in some of the cooler climates. Yes, we infidels can grow this tobacco variety but the special ingredients added in Cuba are a mystery. No one has been able to duplicate the exact flavor of the cigars produced in Cuba. Rumors abound regarding what the Cubans add to give them their special flavor. Suggestions range from the sweat off a cigar maker's brow to manure or maybe even a little "wacky weed" for a kicker. Pepper may also be one of the ingredients, but all we can do is speculate.

Connecticut Broadleaf

Connecticut Broadleaf can be planted in a sunnier location than what's needed for its shade cousin. This variety has very high nicotine content. You should pinch the top out to develop thicker stems and shorter plants for maximum nicotine content. Use this variety for cigars or cigarettes.

Connecticut Shade

Connecticut Shade is a very tall grower and, in fact, it may be the tallest variety. The upper leaves will make great cigar wrappers if you use shade cloth or cheesecloth over your plants to encourage the leaves to be thinner and to keep the bugs off. Plant Connecticut Shade early in the season in areas of the Deep South so you can harvest them before the pressures of insect attacks and summer heat stress build.

Indian Ceremonial Tobacco

Also sold as Original Wild (*Nicotiana rustica*), this is a small, slow-growing species that is quick to flower so you will need to pinch the flower buds out of the top. It is a very harsh tobacco but it does make a nice ornamental type. It's not very good for much else unless you want to experience a Native American peace pipe ceremony. There is a reason their pipes have very long stems and that is because of how harsh this type can be.

Kentucky Burley

Kentucky Burley did well in my garden. I did not smoke cure it but the leaves made a nice blend. It had thicker, stickier leaves that, for me, did not turn as golden of a color as some of the bright Virginia types when the leaves matured.

These represent the varieties I grew in my Fairhope, Alabama, garden in the summer I tested them. There are many more types available on the market. These all did fairly well in my garden but the Virginia Gold #1 was the best performer and provided the nicest golden leaves. The Indian Ceremonial and Narrow Leaf Madole varieties were the poorest performers.

Shopping for the seed is a series of personal decisions you must make based on where you live and what you plan on doing with your harvest. I found that cigarettes and pipe tobacco can be made from blends of all parts of every variety. When you create the blends you will learn how much of each you should allot in the blend. The Virginia Gold #1 also made good cigar wrappers from some of its upper leaves. The cigar types will not turn as golden of a color and tend to have slightly thicker leaves. I found it interesting that the same Virginia Gold #1 seedlings I shared with my friend in Dahlonega (located in north Georgia) had much thicker leaves and thicker stems than the plants I grew in southern Alabama. He had heavy clay soil and I had heavily amended sandy soil. He had very cool nights in the 50s for much of the season and cooler days in the 70s. I had warm nights in the 80s and daytime temperatures in the 90s from late May onward.

You will need to follow the seed company's recommendation for the type to buy for your desired end use and for your geographic location. I found this process to be easy and fun with

Smoking Stats

- 20.6% of all adults (46.6 million people)
- 21.3% of African American adults
- 23.2% of American Indian/Alaska Native adults
- 12.0% of Asian American adults
- 14.5% of Hispanic adults
- 22.1% of white adults

The cigarette industry spends billions each year on advertising and promotions.

- $12.5 billion total spent in 2006
- $34 million a day spent in 2006

the anticipation of how the crop was going to take shape. I recommend buying several varieties from a few different sources the first year, and take good notes of which ones did the best in your garden so you can refine your future decisions.

ORGANIC GROWING FOR THE HOME GARDENER

4

THE BEST FERTILIZER IS YOUR OWN FOOTSTEPS. THIS IS AN IDIOM BUT, OF COURSE, AS A STATEMENT IT IS SO TRUE. YOU MUST CHECK ON YOUR PLANTS REGULARLY IN ORDER TO SUCCEED AT GROWING ANYTHING. THIS APPLIES TO THE SEEDLING STAGE ALL THE WAY THROUGH THE DRYING PROCESS. YOU CANNOT MAKE THE OBVIOUS AND SIMPLE CHANGES THAT THE PLANTS NEED IF YOU DO NOT CHECK ON THEM.

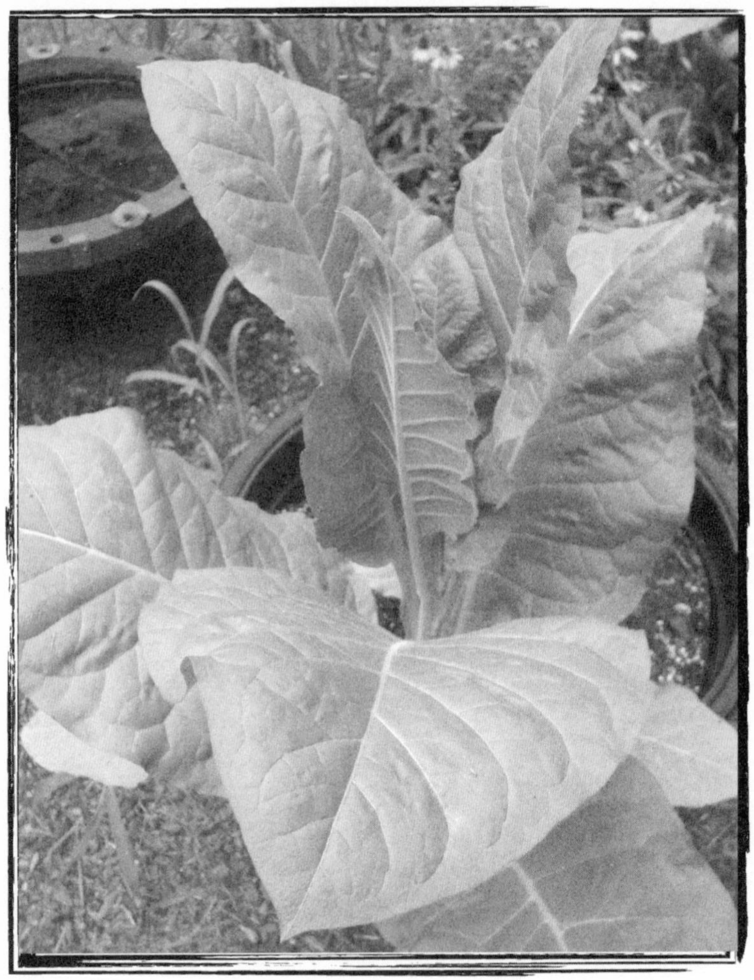

Make checking on your plants a part of your daily routine, just like brushing your teeth. The benefits are many: you will recognize bug problems early in the process; you will see if plants are dry; you will turn off the automatic water system because it rained that night; you will move your seedlings to a sunnier spot because they are starting to stretch for light.

Tips to Help You Plan and Prepare

The best gardens are planned in advance and planted on time. A plant's best growth happens early in the season before it gets scalding hot. If you plant your seedlings indoors early and transplant them to the garden or outdoor containers right after your frost-free date, it makes a big difference. Other tips include:

- Take the time during winter to shop for your seed.
- Get a soil test.
- Start turning your soil well in advance of your planting date (for those of us who don't have frozen ground in winter). Start preparing in the fall if you can.
- Start collecting large outdoor containers if you are planning on gardening in containers.
- Shop for an irrigation system and plan how you are going to water your plants.
- Write out your garden plan in a notebook. Step-by-step as you go through the next few chapters, you can formulate an approach. Follow this plan and mark it on a calendar. Give yourself deadlines for starting seed and planting outside.
- List the supplies you'll need, and buy a few at a time.
- Save the ashes from your fireplace or ask your neighbors to save them for you. You will need this to amend your soil to provide potassium and other minerals.

Tell Your Friends

You will be surprised how quickly you'll find some compatriots in the garden just by mentioning you're growing it to a few fellow smokers. Make growing tobacco a social thing. Your friends may be willing to help. Your neighbors may check on the tobacco while you are gone for the weekend. You may even want to start some friendly competition. Seeds are not expensive, and it is easy to start a few extra plants to give away. You can even have a party come planting time. Weeding is a bit harder to recruit helpers for, but whether you tackle it alone or it becomes a neighborhood competition, a community approach will really make growing more enjoyable. For those of you who live in isolated areas or just don't like your neighbors, there are numerous chat rooms you can visit about tobacco growing to ask advice or just to share your experiences.

Keep a Simple Journal

Make sure you write down what you have done; this can be in a journal (see sample journal, page 156) or just by taking notes. It will help you next season by reminding you of anything you may want to improve or duplicate. You don't have to write down every day's chores but at a minimum write down the date you started the seed, when you transplanted, what you have added

★ ★ ★ ★ ★ ★ ★ ★ ★ ★ ★ ★ ★ ★ ★ ★

Three Basic Tobacco Growing Facts

1. **From seed to smoke, expect the growing and curing process to take about 90 days: 35 to 40 days from seed to transplanting in the garden and 50 to 80 more days to harvest (depending on type). You may be picking a few lower leaves earlier.**

2. **Tobacco growing is very similar to growing tomatoes. That is: lots of sunlight; rich, well-drained soil; and planting on time are the keys to success.**

3. **The methods and information in this chapter apply in general to growing just about any thing. And remember this motto—"Happy Gardening"—for fun and enjoyment.**

to the soil, where in the garden the different plants were, how you fertilized, and when you harvested. This will become a valuable reference tool and, at the very least, provide something to help you remember your experience.

How Much Sun Is Needed?

Six to eight hours of direct sunlight is good. You can have filtered shade, but deep shade underneath a giant tree will slow the plants' growth too much. The more shade, the more thinner bodied and spindly the leaves will be. Keep in mind that more sun also means more water. Tobacco grown for cigar wrappers, which is the highest grade, is usually grown under 30 percent shade cloth. (Shade cloth blocks out some of the sun's rays.) Farmers prefer white shade cloth to black shade cloth. In sunnier areas of the country, a location that gets some afternoon shade is ideal.

Good Soil is the Key

Why Not Just Plant in Dirt?

Okay, back to the garden for a talk about soil. Good soil is something you can grow plants in and dirt, well, dirt is good for foundations, roads, and filling in holes. Dirt is meant to be packed down and has none of the organic matter or air space that is so crucial for plants to thrive.

You will need to have a location that does not stand in water. If standing water is a problem that means your soil is poorly drained, and you should consider using raised beds or containers. A raised bed is literally a bed made on top of your regular soil; basically, it's a large box that you fill with good topsoil or a potting soil mix to control poor drainage or poor soils in general. Raised beds are often made using rocks, timbers, or boards. The "bible" of raised bed gardening, *All New Square Foot Gardening*, was written by Mel Bartholomew (Cool Springs Press, 2006). Here's a drainage test: if you are planting in the ground, dig a hole about 2 feet deep, and fill it with water.

If it takes longer than 8 hours for the water to drain away, you probably have slow-draining soil.

The highest quality tobacco is grown in well-drained soil. It will have the right amount of potash and be rich in mineral nutrients. These soils will typically be dark and crumbly; ideally, the soil will not have been cultivated for several years. While sandy soils typically do not grow as high of a grade of tobacco, they will work if you add great deal of compost, lime, and potash to amend them. Heavy clay soils will need to be turned over deeply and also need lots of added compost.

Healthy, rich soil that drains well and has not been cultivated for decades (if ever) is known as virgin soil; finding virgin soil now usually involves clearing land. In the past, farmers would use recently cleared land because the forest floor was covered in "compost" after years of leaf matter had built up on it. Because of those leaves rotting and the lack of compaction, virgin soil is naturally productive without needing a great deal of amendments. Compaction is the process by which the ground is packed down and made rock hard either by the use of heavy equipment or even from the effects of rainfall on exposed soil. The goal is to have soil that is not compacted; it should be crumbly and able to be easily worked with a shovel. Also, if you are not one of the blessed few who have great soil naturally, then you will need to add compost and ashes from your fireplace (which is potash). However, unless you plan to clear some land, you will need to learn about composting.

Composting Is the Great Soil Builder

You must have or create good soil to be a successful grower. If you are growing in the ground (versus in containers) some advance work will pay big dividends later. The goal is to have around 20 percent of any soil be from composted organic matter. I cannot overstress how important composting is and how important adding it to the garden can be to the garden's long-term health. Becoming competent at composting and taking advantage of the raw materials you have on hand will become a badge of honor as you grow as a gardener. You need to know the difference between composted material and uncomposted material. The difference between finished and raw compost is that finished compost has decomposed and raw compost has not. This is important because if you mix something into the soil that has not decomposed, such as raw grass clippings or fresh pine bark, you may do more harm than good.

Compost can be from many different sources. Native Americans would bury a fish under each plant they planted and let the fish decompose to provide nutrients. Cow manure makes great compost, and it's readily available. I usually do not recommend chicken manure because chickens can't kill weed seeds as they go through their gut. The chicken manure usually has nitrogen levels that are too high too. Plus, non-organic chicken farmers use a great deal of copper and antibiotics in the feed that the chickens are fed; personally, I don't recommend that.

Homemade compost can be made from grass clippings and leaves. You will need a mixture of green (fresh) and brown (dried) yard clippings and leaves. You can also add left-over vegetable kitchen scraps but be careful to avoid meat or meat byproducts (including fats) as they will attract vermin. Time and turning the pile are keys to great composting. The less time you have, the more often you will need to turn the compost piles. You can even buy commercial compost bins, which are like plastic balls or tumblers, to allow you to easily and frequently turn the mix into "black gold" in a matter of weeks.

Black gold is a great term for compost because it best describes the finished product you are looking for. Good compost will be crumbly in texture and have a rich, dark color when it's finished.

Part of the magic of composting is that you can actually feel or observe the heat that the internal or middle part of the pile produces; the pile will "steam" under certain conditions. Or, you may want to purchase a long-stemmed thermometer to monitor this heat. Heat occurs when the microbes go to work breaking down organic matter. Microbes are the engines that drive the compost train. Your pile should be hot enough to sterilize the compost; that temperature is around 180 degrees.

I have seen large commercial piles of fresh pine bark actually get hot enough to catch on fire inside a compost pile! Internal heat also speeds up the process of breaking everything down. The "right" amount of moisture is needed to help the microbes go to work. Moisture can be in the form of water from the hose or from adding green material (which naturally has more moisture in it). You will know you have added enough green matter to the compost pile when you see steam as you turn the pile. An 80:20 ratio of brown to green material is a typical proportion. The goal when building a compost pile is to create the conditions for the living microbes to thrive.

You will need to control the moisture levels in your compost pile. You do not want a nasty, sopping wet pile and you do not want a bone-dry pile, either. If it is on the dry side add a little water, especially when you turn it. If you have been getting heavy rains place a tarp over the top of the pile. If you are in an arid or dry climate you will need to add water. If you live in an area where the temperatures are above freezing for a relatively short period of time you will need to use every means necessary to speed up the process to home compost or plan on purchasing it in a bagged form. (This means people living in the Rockies and similar climates.) Composting can become a hobby and an art form in itself. It is easy and with some practice you can become one of the "compost clan."

Compost can be purchased in bags. I have had good luck over the years amending with the Black Cow® brand found in

Build Your Own Compost Bin

A common composting method is to build simple bins from lumber and wire in order to have piles that are deep enough for heat to build up. These bins will have wooden or wire sides and posts on the corners for support. They can be anything from old wooden pallets to finely crafted wooden corrals. These compost bins range from 5 feet by 5 feet square, 3 or 4 feet tall, to ones so large they require a tractor with a scoop to turn the piles. Three bins are usually used so there is sequence to the composting: fresh material is piled in the first bin and then turned and flipped over to the second bin after a certain amount of time. That amount of time will vary depending on the temperature, moisture levels, and materials you are composting. Higher amounts of green matter and the right amount of moisture, as well running the material through a shredder (to make smaller bits), will all speed up the process. The final flip-and-turn is from the second to the third bin. After this last bin goes through its heat cycle you should have compost that is crumbly and broken down enough to enrich the soil. While it's not absolutely necessary, some people mix in a little lime or wood ashes each time they turn the pile. You should try composting as part of the process of growing your own tobacco. You will learn to work with the raw materials on hand and develop your own personal composting system.

the yellow bags at most retail garden centers across the country. Not suprisingly, considering its name, Black Cow is composted cow manure. For the purists, there is also a brand called Black Treasure® that can be found online; it is made from the manure of Angus cows fed organic feed. There is also worm castings compost, which is great when you can find it. You can often buy bulk composted pine bark from your local garden center or landscape supply yard; just make sure it is not too fresh before you dig it into the ground. A shovelful of compost for every five shovelsful of soil when you double dig your garden is a generous amount and will add the needed nutrients, except potash or potassium, for an entire season. Many types of compost can be purchased online if you cannot readily find it sold in your area.

Amending with compost also will buffer or adjust the alkalinity or acidity of your garden. The levels of alkalinity or acid in soil are noted by its pH level, which ranges from 0 to 14. A pH of 7 is neutral (neither alkaline nor acid). If your soil is too acidic (less than 7) then it will raise the pH. If your soil tests basic with a high pH (way over 7) then compost will lower the pH. The target pH of tobacco is 6.2. Without getting too technical, compost is the great fertilizer and equalizer to make a perfect garden for tobacco (or whatever you are growing). Testing pH levels is really pretty easy; you just submit a sample to your local County Extension office, pay a small fee, and you

will get a report indicating the pH (and other important criteria) about your in-ground soil. Check online for your local office of the Extension service. Testing pH isn't really necessary if you're growing in containers because you are controlling the growing medium 100 percent.

Crop Rotation and Cover Crops

Sustainable agriculture is the practice of using farming techniques that build healthy soil instead of depleting the nutrients, which means becoming dependent on chemical fertilizers, which in turn results in dead soil over time. Practicing crop rotation and planting cover crops are keys to sustainable agriculture.

Tobacco is a heavy user of nitrogen and potassium and sucks a great deal of these nutrients from the soil. So you will need to grow tobacco in a different area each season if you are growing in the ground. Never plant tobacco in an area that had tomatoes within the last five years because of the risk of transmitting disease (from the tomatoes to the tobacco). Ideally, if you are rotating crops in the garden and don't have the luxury of virgin soil, you would sow a crop of tobacco after one of onions or radishes because they are in plant families that are completely different from tobacco. Plants that are in the same families can transmit diseases more easily than plants that are in different plant families.

Planting "cover crops" of legumes will also build your soil. Cover crops are plants you seed in winter and fall between sowing your main crops. You don't want garden soil to sit exposed as bare dirt in winter because any rain will compact the soil and weeds will move in. These cover crops are also referred to as "green manures." Legumes are a class of plants that have nodules in their roots that actually convert nitrogen from the air and store it in their roots. Clover, soybeans, crown vetch, and cowpeas are all legumes. Planting clover in fall and rotating soybeans as part of your crop rotation will lessen the dependence on chemical fertilizers and build healthy soils at the same time. (This may not affect a backyard tobacco grower as much, but this is especially important if you farm on a larger scale and don't have access to large amounts of compost or cow manure.) My great-uncle Frederick Dugger started the original rotation experiment at Auburn University's campus in 1896. By using cover crops and rotating legume types, that test farmland is still one of the most productive pieces of land in the country—all without relying on large amounts of chemical fertilizers. The crop rotation is cotton, crimson clover, wheat, vetch, oats, corn, rye, cowpeas, soybeans, and then cotton again on a four-year rotation. If you ever visit the campus at Auburn University in Auburn, Alabama, look for this land behind the girls' dorm on "The Hill." It is the longest ongoing university farming experiment in the United States.

Soil Preparation: Getting the Garden Ready

Soil Test

Getting a soil test is easy and a great way to get started with growing your own tobacco. This can be done in fall or in spring. Your County Extension agent, as well as your local garden centers, will have little boxes you'll need in order to gather soil samples. All you have to do is dig a few soil samples from around your garden and send it to the testing lab address noted on the box. Usually the samples will be sent to the land grant university in your state. This is usually a free or very inexpensive service. The soil test results will give you specific instructions on what your soil needs and, in particular, how much lime, potash, or percentage of organic matter is needed for the optimum growing conditions.

Turn the Garden Soil

"Turning" the garden soil means to plow deeply with a tiller or tractor or dig trenches with a shovel and throw the soil over on itself, which effectively turns the soil. Ideally, turning the soil is done in fall and then again in spring a few weeks before you plant. In the same ideal world, you would add lime and potash after the initial plowing. You'll then plow or turn it again, mixing in the amendments that you've added to create a nice seedbed. Then you plant crown vetch or crimson clover or another cover crop to set the stage for your spring planting. In spring, you should then plow or otherwise turn under the cover crop.

Next, make the beds and rows just like you want them, evenly spaced with a lower trench or furrow 2 to 4 feet apart and the raised lines of the beds following the shape of the land to create terraces for soil and water conservation. You may not

Soil Tip

Here's how to tell if the soil is too wet: take a handful of soil and squeeze it in the palm of your hand. If it sticks together when you unclasp your palm, then it's too wet.

have the equipment like a tiller, tractor, or plow this first season to do each of these steps and lay out terraces, but if you plan to grow tobacco or garden on a larger scale, this should be part of your garden plan. (Of course, if you are growing just a plant or two, you don't have to do this.)

A soil preparation method used by the small home gardener that is very common is called "double digging," a practice dating to medieval times. This is where you'd dig a trench 18 to 24 inches deep, moving the soil from the first trench to the side, and then dig another trench alongside the first. Fill the first trench with the soil from the second trench and so forth for as many trenches as you're digging until you have turned each row in the garden to a depth double that of a shovel. When you come to the last row, move the soil from the first trench into it. Make the trenches the spacing you want between your rows. These will become your beds. This deep turning gives plant roots plenty of room to grow and will break up any compacted soil. You should also remove any weed roots or bulbs you see. You will want to add compost, lime, and potash at this point. Remember, a shovelful of compost for every five shovelsful of soil is a good rule of thumb.

A very important thing to remember and pay attention to is that, particularly with clay soils, you cannot plow or turn the ground when it is too wet or too dry. When the soil is too dry you will work twice as hard. If the soil is too wet you will make clods and ruin the soil structure. You can get away with working the soil if it's too dry when planting in sandier or looser soils but never turn any soil when it is sopping wet. You may very well turn it into a texture that's just like concrete.

Lime

Most soils in the United States benefit from the addition of lime. Lime is derived from crushed limestone, and it is available in a powder or pelletized form; personally, I like the pelletized form. But if the soil pH needs to be raised more than 1.0 in a single year, you might want to use the powder; it's more reactive and will have a faster effect. Dolomitic lime also adds calcium and magnesium. Your soil test will tell you exactly how much is needed but without a test, a 50 pound bag spread over 1,000 square feet is a safe amount (prorate this for smaller areas). Lime works best when applied in fall but it can be applied a few weeks before planting. The purpose of the lime is to raise the alkalinity and buffer the pH

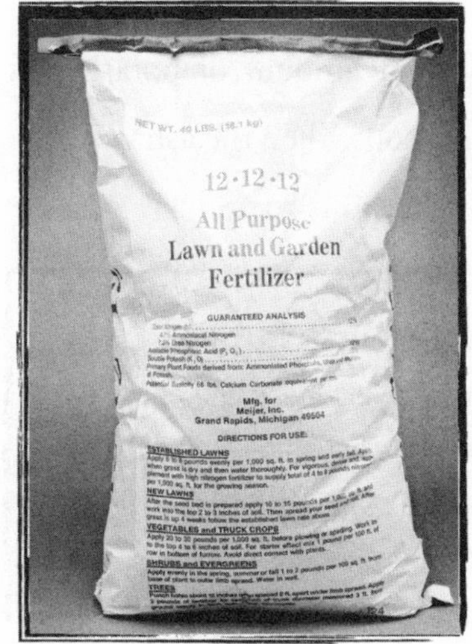

level of the soil, and lime must be turned into the soil—not just applied on top of the ground.

Potash

The fertilizer abbreviation of "NPK" stands for nitrogen, phosphorus, and potassium. Potash contains high levels of potassium, which is represented by the letter "K" on the periodic table. Potash is very important for tobacco growing in particular. The word "potash" is derived from the time when people kept ashes from their household fires in a metal pot ("pot" + "ash"). Potash now comes in several forms. It is most readily available for the small garden in the form of ashes from hardwood or even charcoal fires. Traditionally, farmers who had small plots of tobacco would actually build fires in fall and winter on the spots where they were going to grow their crop. This was to sterilize the top of the soil, kill the weeds, and to add the ashes to the soil. The highest amount of potash was created when farmers burned corncobs. Then the ash would be tilled into the soil. A good rule of thumb is to add 1½ pounds of potash for every 100 square feet. Potash is also found in crushed granite, kelp meal, alfalfa compost, and greensand. Kelp meal is good and can be used is small quantities. It is readily found on

Protection Tip

When applying these fine powders, be sure to wear some type of protective mask, as they can be harmful to your lungs.

the West Coast and can be ordered online. Greensand is mined in the northeastern United States and is the residue or mineral deposits left by crustaceans and similar creatures when the earth was covered by ocean. The application rate for greensand is 5 to 10 pounds per 100 square feet. The easiest source of potash to acquire is the ashes from a fire, so remember to save them in your ashcan.

Buying Seed and Starting Seedlings

Tobacco seed is relatively inexpensive, and the trays for growing seedlings are not really expensive either; expect to spend about 30 dollars or so. If you have never grown seedlings before, this is a relatively easy process. Germination rates (the percentage of the seed that will come up) for tobacco are generally good, and you should expect them all to emerge in a week or so depending on temperatures.

The first step is buying the seed. I found several great sources online for the home gardener, from organic open-pollinated seed to named varieties both old and modern—it is all there. I planted Virginia Gold #1, Havana, Louisiana Perique, Indian Ceremonial tobacco, Burley Original, and Narrow Leaf Madole. You must decide the type of tobacco you want to grow based on whether you want to have cigarette, pipe, cigar, or chewing tobacco. It is good to be able to blend the different types. Very often the taste of tobacco depends on the grade of the leaf when it was harvested and how well it is dried and cured. The most important thing is to try several different types your first time growing to find the ones that grow best in your conditions and climate and that are to your taste. Sources that I used include Heirloom Organics, Victory Heirloom Seed Company, The Tobacco Seed Company, Seedman.com, and New Hope Seed Company. In the closing pages these are all listed with their full contact information.

Starting Transplants

Start transplants in winter six weeks or so before your area's last expected frost. The best way to decide when to start seed is to

look up your area's average frost-free date (the expected date of the last frost). Using that date, count backward on a calendar to calculate the number of weeks that your transplants will need to mature enough in order to be ready to plant outside by that frost-free date. Seed will need to be sown indoors in flats or outside in cold frames against a heated building.

For indoor growing you will need trays, some type of light source, and fine seedling mix potting soil. I purchased Jiffy® trays with domes and used the Jiffy® seedling mix for the potting soil, and I was very happy with the results. These are available at your local garden retailers and home-improvement stores. These were very easy to use and very forgiving. The plastic dome prevents the seedlings from drying out too fast, and you can leave them a few days at a time if you go out of town. Be careful not to put a tray with the dome on it in full sun because it can overheat. But the seedlings will grow too tall or stretch if you put them in a dark area. Monitor the Jiffy® trays just as you would a cold frame outside, where you raise or remove the lid to allow air to circulate on warm sunny days and close the lid at night and on rainy, cold days after the seedlings begin to grow.

You will also need to use plant labels if you are growing more than one type of tobacco. Believe me, you will be happy you labeled them, because you absolutely will not remember which tray is which. Transplants can also be grown outside in cold frames positioned against the house, in a basement under fluorescent light, or in a sunny spot indoors. Use new sterile fine-textured potting soil from a recently purchased bag for this first stage of growing. A new bag will not have weed seed or disease issues and the smaller particle size of the media (potting soil) will allow the seedlings to get a good start.

Cold Frames

If you have one, a cold frame is very handy. A cold frame basically is a four-sided enclosure with clear lids (or windows) that open and shut. They are usually built 2 or 3 feet tall and have compartments that are 6 feet by 4 feet. On sunny, warm days you manage them by opening the lids a bit to keep them from getting too hot (over 85 degrees F) and prop them open with a stick. The concept is that on colder or cloudy days, the lids should remain closed to retain heat and moisture. Cold frames are best used in milder climates and even then they work best when located next to a heated building on its sunniest side for the maximum results. Cold frames use the radiant energy from the sun for heat. Cold frames are typically used if you are starting larger amounts of seed for a small farm or large garden.

Sowing the Seed

For the less-experienced gardener, here are a few definitions that I'll use in this section: the word "sowing" means the act of spreading the seed on the trays, and "seedlings" are the name for the very young plants.

First, lightly water the sterile fine seedling potting soil until it is just moist. You want it wet but not to the point that you can squeeze water when you pick up a handful. Just add a little water at a time—not too soggy! Fill the tray with the seedling potting soil until it's one-half inch or so from the top.

The rule of thumb for tobacco is to never, ever cover the seed. You want to just sprinkle seeds on top of the potting mix in the tray and keep that top layer just moist. The plastic domes I used prevented me from having to water much, but if you do need to water, only apply a fine mist from a spray bottle to avoid washing the seed away.

Tobacco seeds are very small and will come up and grow too closely together if they are just dumped in the tray in a mass. The seeds can be mixed with fine, clean sand like play sand or builders sand to make them easier to space them out in the seedling tray. You can also buy a little plastic trowel that has a "clicker" built into the handle that's designed specifically for seeding that will measure them out. The idea is that, for each click, a seed drops off the end of the trowel into the seedbed. But if you can find it, pelletized seed (used by commercial growers) is worth seeking out. Seeds can be sown thickly but that just makes it harder to separate them later when you transplant them. You can also carefully sprinkle the seed on the top of the seed tray and spread them apart to the correct spacing. This takes a very steady hand and a fair amount of patience.

You will need to fertilize your seedlings during these early stages while they are in the seed trays. Potting soil typically does not have any fertilizer in it, and it does not retain nutrients, so nutrients must be added. A capful or two of fish emulsion added to the watering can every few times you water will be enough. (This is considered a low rate of fertilization.) You will not need to fertilize until after the plants start to develop their second set of leaves. Tobacco seedlings are very susceptible to fertilizer salts injury until they are established with at least one set of true leaves. The set of double leaves you see are called the "seed leaves." The next set of two leaves

you will see are the first "true leaves." You will want to grow seedlings in their trays for three weeks or so, depending on temperature and light levels, until they are ready to transplant. They will not need any water for the first week or two and very little after that. Remember: use a fine mist if you have to water at all early on or you will wash the tiny seeds away. It is not until they are growing that they will actually need any water.

One thing that can happen during the seedling stage if the seedlings are watered late in the day and the leaves and stems stay wet all night (with visible water droplets on them) is a disease called "damping off." This is when the stem rots right at the soil level, and the first sign is a bad case of dying followed by a terminal case of dead. The disease is called Rhizoctonia, and it will also cause the plants to yellow. If you start to see signs of damping off, back off on the watering and take steps to dry them out a bit. A young seedling is better off being a little too dry than a little too wet. When you're using the plastic-domed seedling trays you will know you have the right amount of moisture when there is just a small amount of condensation in the lid. If you see water droplets form and there are drops visible on the leaves, then take the lid off and put the tray in a dry, sunny spot or near a heater. I put metal cooking pans under my trays so I could move them around to give them more light or dry them out a bit. I moved the trays outside on sunny days to a spot with filtered shade to help them get the maximum growth and toughen them up a bit in preparation for transplanting. By "toughening up" I mean that I exposed the young seedlings to stronger light, wind, outside air and the conditions they will have to grow in once they are ready to be transplanted to the outside world. You start with putting seedlings out for a short while (maybe a hour or so), and gradually increase the time they are exposed to the outdoor elements. This is also called "hardening off."

Transplanting

Transplanting is the act of taking the seedlings and planting them in small pots. The seedlings are then called "transplants." Your tobacco seedlings will be ready to transplant to small pots once they have developed two or three sets of leaves.

Here how to do it: Fill the small pots with clean, new sterile potting soil and transplant the baby seedlings into them.

I placed the small pots in plastic trays to make them easier to handle. You will want to put them in a shady spot at first to avoid transplant shock. Transplant shock happens when a seedling is moved to a new environment; it's easily burned or wilts due to the damage done by taking them out of their first pot and moving them to the larger pots. Handle the young seedlings carefully; some people use a spoon or toothpick to get the baby seedlings out of their seedling tray. It is wise to poke a hole in the top of the potting soil in the small pot were the plant is going with a pencil or your finger and then place the seedling roots in. Then gently press the potting soil around the seedling to close the hole after you insert the plant.

Your goal is to plant seedlings at the same depth they were growing in the seed tray. Be sure to water them well after they

are planted to finish closing up the holes you made in the media and to settle any extra air spaces in the soil. This is called "watering in" and it is important.

Keep the transplants in a shady spot the first day so they can recover. You will then need to increase their exposure to light until they are ready for full outdoor sun in the garden. Two or three days to get them ready is enough time. Start out with a few hours of morning sun the first day, then add a few hours to the afternoon the next day, and then on the third day give them a few more hours until they are "toughened up" and ready to plant.

Transplants receiving too little light will stretch (just what it sounds like), looking for the sun just like seedlings. It is hard for seedlings or transplants to recover from stretching, because they will have a weak stem. It is not the end if they stretch but if you notice seedlings starting to get pale, weak, and too tall, you should give them more light and a little less water and fertilizer. You want them to develop a stem strong enough to stand up to watering, wind, and rain when they go outside. However, don't ever keep seedlings or transplants in total darkness. Towards the end of this stage, you will actually want to move them outside on sunny warm days if you can. This is called "hardening off" or "toning" them. The tobacco transplants growing in small pots will need four or five weeks of growing time before they are sturdy enough and have a root system that's developed enough to plant in the ground or containers outside in direct sunlight.

I prefer to transplant seedlings to small Jiffy® peat pots so there is less transplant shock when they go into the garden. If you use plastic pots, you'll have to wait for the roots to grow out to the edge or well enough for them to hold together when you remove the pot. The ease of using a peat pot is you can plant everything—pot and all—into the ground with little or no transplant shock. You don't have to wait for the roots to grow out either. Just make sure the top edge of the peat pot is covered by soil or compost. Otherwise, the peat pot will act like a wick to suck moisture out of the container potting soil.

When you transplant a seedling from the seedbed, cold frame, or starter tray and then again from the small pots to the garden, there is the chance that they will go into shock due to the damage that is done to the roots, no matter how careful you are. Signs of transplant shock include wilting and burning. Transplant shock can be avoided with a few simple steps such as transplanting on a cloudy day and allowing a day or so for the seedlings to recover in a shady spot. You will also want to "harden off" the seedlings by increasing their exposure to full sun in the days leading up to transplanting.

Transplants will need more water than your seedlings did and peat pots dry out more quickly than plastic pots do—check them every day, in the mornings and in the afternoons if you can, to see if they need water. As they grow, their water need will continue to increase. The transplants should be fertilized once a week with a liquid fish emulsion added to the watering can; just follow the instructions on the label for the rate (ratio of fertilizer to water).

If you planted the seeds in a cold frame and if you spaced them far enough apart you can skip the transplanting into small pots stage. Just let the seedlings grow, and then transplant them directly into the garden after they are hardened off or toned for the sun. If you live in an area with very long growing seasons you can also plant the seed directly in the garden. This is called "direct sowing." I only recommend this in areas that have mild summers; otherwise, you want to give the plants a head start on the hot part of the summer by growing seedlings.

Transplanting to the Garden or to Containers

Just as you were careful to transplant your seedlings on a cloudy or overcast day, you should do the same when transplanting in small pots to the garden or patio container. In the garden, ideally, you will have already turned under compost and the last additives several weeks ahead of time, and you should have begun preparations in the area the previous fall.

The plants will need to be spaced 2 feet apart and, depending on your space and personal preference, there should be about 3 or 4 feet between the rows. The reason you'd want wider rows is to give yourself room to work when tending the

beds and picking the leaves. Plant them in rows of soil that have been laid out so that there are two "levels"—the lower areas are between rows and the planting beds have been made a bit higher on the actual row. Take care not to bury the transplants deeper than they were already growing. If you did not add enough organic matter or are growing in containers, you will need to supplement with liquid feedings. Do not begin this process until the plants have begun to grow, usually in a week or two, and have had time to establish some new roots.

Tobacco is a notoriously poorly rooted crop. It's planted on raised beds and, through successive cultivation, more soil is moved to the bases of the plants to provide more bed into which the roots can grow. It has no tap root so by building a bed, its fibrous roots can attach themselves throughout the soil as the plant increases in size.

The Importance of Mulch

An advantage of gardening on a smaller than commercial scale is that you will be able to add mulch. Mulch is a layer of organic material that is added on top of the soil. This does not need to be compost, but it can be. You can use pine straw, oak leaves, pine nuggets, pine bark, and so forth. Use whatever organic plant material is readily available in your area that does not contain the enemy—weed seed.

Mulching as much as 4 to 6 inches deep is great if you have that much available. You can use compost as a mulch, and it will slowly feed your plants during the season. You can turn under the mulch into the soil at the end of the season after it has broken down (decomposed). If it did not break down during the season then you can simply scrape it off, pile it up, and compost it.

Watering—Not Too Much, Not Too Little

It may sound complicated to the novice (or even experienced) gardener, but the rule is to not water too much, a.k.a. "overwater,"

Mulch Plays Several Important Roles

1. **Mulch keeps the soil from compacting, which is an enemy to root growth.**
2. **Mulch insulates a plant's root system from high temperatures before its leaves shade the soil.**
3. **Mulch slows down weed growth, saving you weeding chores.**
4. **Mulch also aids moisture retention, which is a fancy term for holding in water.**
5. **Mulch keeps water and soil from splashing up onto a plant's lower leaves, which causes diseases to spread and gets dirt on your tobacco plants.**

and don't let plants dry all the way out, or "underwater." The exact amount of water to give plants falls somewhere in-between under- and overwatering. How much to water really depends on your climate and soil conditions. In an ideal scenario, you'd have a great soil that has 20 percent organic matter, the water does not stand when it rains, it holds the perfect amount of moisture, and has a nice thick mulch on top so that it will only need to be watered once a week. If you have sandier soil or are farther south, watering will be necessary more often. Heavy clay soils are great until you get too much rain. It is always easier to add more water than to take it away. When you first set out the transplants they will need to be watered every day for the first couple of weeks, until the roots are established.

Tobacco has two critical periods for adequate watering—during the 3 to 4 weeks after transplanting and after the flowers form. Overwatering at any other time can lead to lower nicotine levels, more oil in the leaf, and a lower quality overall. Some drought stress isn't really a bad thing for quality tobacco (except for the two times mentioned). Overwatered tobacco tends to be thin-bodied and lacks flavor.

There are several different methods you can use to deliver the "right" amount of water. There are drip systems both for in-ground gardens and containers in differing levels of sophistication. I have had great luck with a simple timer and a sprinkler on the end of a hose. You can buy these timers for around 30 dollars, and they attach between the spigot and the hose. The timer can be programmed for the days of the week and how long the run time needs to be. There are simpler ones that are less expensive that just turn the hose on and off. I had to

Watering Tips to Remember

- A method I have found to be extremely effective during the season is to watch the plants, especially when they are young, and water at the first sign of wilt. Wilting is when you see the leaves begin to drop slightly and curl under a bit. By watching, you will learn what a plant's water needs are.
- If you think you are overwatering and mold is growing on the mulch, then you are overwatering.
- After a while, once plants have become established, you can initiate a watering routine if does not rain.
- Plants in containers require more water (because of drainage and evaporation) and may need watering every day.
- Try to avoid watering in the middle of the day when the temperature is over 90 degrees Fahrenheit.
- Do not water so late in the day that you put wet plants to bed at night. This will cause all kinds of disease issues.
- Do not water so much that there is standing water everywhere. This is not only a waste of water, but is also a cause of disease problems.
- When you water, make sure that you are getting the water to a plant's root zone. Thirty minutes to an hour is usually plenty, but scrape around in the ground to see how deeply you are watering. Dig down at least two or three inches.

★ ★ ★ ★ ★ ★ ★ ★ ★ ★ ★

go out of town one time for ten days, and I set my timer to run 30 minutes once a day. It worked fine both for the plants in the containers as well as the ones in the ground. If you have pots or containers on your deck, several retailers sell a very nice drip system that is easy to install. You can also use soaker hoses.

Just remember: whatever you do, avoid sending wet plants to bed at night, and check to see how far down or deeply the water is soaking into the ground.

Fertilizing

This section is meant to guide you through the process of fertilizing and maintaining proper fertility. If you have added enough compost (5 percent by volume is ideal) and potash, or have naturally perfect virgin forest floor soil and have added potash, then your work is done from a fertility standpoint. This will be all that you will probably need for the growing season.

But, if you are growing in containers or pots or have soil that needed some amending (amending is a fancy gardening word for adding compost, lime, potash, and other nutrients), and you did not add mulch or did not add anything at all, then you need to have a plan for supplemental fertilizing.

Fertilizing In General

Tobacco primarily needs nitrogen, and potash in particular, although the flavor and health of tobacco plants are also influenced by other minerals that the plants pull from the soil. The letters on any kind of fertilizer are "NPK" and these three represent the major nutrients that plants need. Each letter is associated with a corresponding number that represents the percentage of that ingredient in the overall fertilizer mix.

The first letter N stands for Nitrogen, the second letter P stands for Phosphorous, and the third letter K stands for Potassium (also called potash). Tobacco plants are considered heavy feeders. Although you can just sprinkle some dry chemical fertilizer on top of the ground (also know as topdressing), this would only help you out for the short term and this practice will eventually ruin the soil. Chemical fertilizers do not produce the same flavor and quality of tobacco that a well amended soil, or organic fertilization process will produce. This same rule also applies broadly to food crops, especially to tomatoes, and even shrubs and trees. If you find you need to add more fertilizer due to early yellowing of the young leaves on seedlings or after the plants are transplanted, you have the option of feeding them through the water hose with a fertilizer siphon injector or a hose-end feeder. (The hose-end feeders are called that because you attach them to the end of a hose.) They are fairly inexpensive and for less than 30 dollars you can liquid feed your tobacco plants. Again, yes, you can use Miracle Grow® or some other type of chemical liquid fertilizer, just don't overdo it, or, even worse, apply it late in the season. I prefer the organic methods and use organic fertilizers such as fish emulsion and Terra Cycle®.

The fertilizer siphon injector I mention is easily found online or at local garden centers. You simply screw the end onto a spigot or hose, stick a tube in a bucket with your fish emulsion or compost tea, and it will meter (measure) the liquid fertilizer into the sprinkler, drip line, soaker hose, or hand wand. It is easy to use and is less than 20 dollars. Make sure you use the one with a back-flow preventer. A back-flow preventer is another simple, inexpensive device that keeps fluids from being sucked back in to the line contaminating your drinking water. Modern siphon injectors have these built-in already.

Compost tea can be made by placing compost in some hosiery (which has been tied off on the ends) and allowing it to steep in the sun in a bucket or barrel full of water. I supplement it by adding fish emulsion. This works well in large drums for small-scale farming or large gardens and is added to the irrigation with the siphon injector.

If you feel like you must use chemical fertilizers, then follow the rate prescribed by your soil sample or on the fertilizer bag itself. Be careful not to purchase any fertilizer with weed killer in it; weed killer is an herbicide (and herbicides will kill plants).

After a tobacco plant has about 8 to 12 leaves, do not provide any supplemental fertilizer. It will soon be time to harvest and too much feeding too late in the game will affect leaf quality. Also, don't supply any supplemental feed until two weeks after transplanting.

Different Types Need Different Things

Different tobacco types are fertilized differently. Flue-cured (and Oriental types) should be fertilized early, when plants have 10 leaves, and then allowed to "run out" of nitrogen for the best quality. Overfertilizing with nitrogen will lead to over-ripe tobacco that does not cure well and will be low quality.

Burley, dark, and Perique types are big users of nitrogen; they should be more heavily fertilized. The whole plant will be harvested at once when the lower leaves show some nitrogen deficiency. Dark types like Narrow Leaf Madole will not usually turn yellow on the bottom leaves from nitrogen deficiency when they are ready for harvest, so keep that in mind.

Nitrogen is the most important component to fertilizing tobacco, and it should be adjusted for different types. There can be too much of a good thing; overfertilization means the tobacco leaves are difficult to cure, usually of poor quality, and will produce a harsh quality when smoked. Tobacco is a "luxury" user of potassium, meaning that overfertilizing with potassium doesn't influence quality—you just have to have enough of it.

Tobacco uses relatively little of the minor nutrients. Chlorine is one that can adversely affect the burning quality of tobacco. Tobacco watered with excessive chlorine will not burn well. This should be kept in mind when using city water that's high in chlorine.

Growing in Containers

If you plan on growing tobacco in containers, you will use a commercial potting mix (you use this instead of regular soil). These mixes typically are made up of a mixture of peat moss, pine bark, and perlite. The perlite is basically like small pieces of Styrofoam™ added to maintain room for air spaces inside the container. Roots have to have air space in order to "breathe;" it's essential. Mix in 5 percent or so by volume of composted manure such as Black Cow®, worm compost, Black Steer®, or

something similar to these products to provide some natural nutrients for your tobacco plants. (Composted is a term that I covered in detail in a previous section, but it basically means "broken down.")

You also need to add some potash to the mix. For containers you can mix in a little greensand or wood ashes. My tobacco grown in containers all did well using Sungro® commercial potting soil, which I purchased at my local garden center. Large home & garden retailers and garden centers sell great potting soil mixes.

I also kept my containers fed with a liquid fish emulsion once a week or so during the season until it was close to time to harvest. Fish emulsion is readily available and you can mix it in a watering can, sprinkle it on, or use a hose-end mixer or siphon injector just like I described for use in the garden. Just follow the instructions on the label. Some friends of mine grew their tobacco containers nicely using Osmocote® slow-release fertilizer; however, it is non-organic and you may overfeed if it releases too fast. Just use the low rate written on the fertilizer bag. An option is not to use slow-release fertilizers at all; too much nitrogen at the end of the growing season will result in overripe tobacco, especially flue-cured types.

Although you can grow a decent plant in a five-gallon pot, it won't get as big; ten-gallon-sized pots or larger work best. When you fill the pots with potting medium, don't fill them all the way to the rim in order to leave some room when you water.

Tobacco plants grown in containers may need staking in a fashion similar to the way tomatoes are staked. You can use bamboo or wooden stakes 4 to 5 feet tall; tie the stalks to the stakes loosely with twine. Believe it or not, tobacco makes a great ornamental centerpiece in a container mixed with flowers. You can mix it with herbs like mint or with marigolds to repel bugs like you would do in the garden. Just use plants that also like the same conditions; that is, that like the same amount of water and can take the sun. SunPatiens® make great companion plants, as will geraniums and vinca if you want to dress up your patio or deck. Add some trailing plants to the edge like creeping jenny to help hide the container. Just note that adding the flowers or herbs will increase the amount of water that you will need to provide.

Tobacco grown in a container all by itself will use more water than in the ground. You should plan on watering every day until water runs out of the bottom of the pot in hot climates. At the very least, position the container to have easy access to a hose because you will be using it a great deal. Just like I recommend for the garden, there are some very simple drip systems available. Many retail garden centers and do-it-yourself home stores carry drip systems made especially for containers. There are also several timers you can use to simplify things; just remember to check on your plants to make sure the little emitters (a fancy word for the place where the water comes out of the tube on a drip system) are not clogged.

TOBACCO DISEASES AND PESTS, AND THEIR CONTROLS

5

A FOCUS ON HEALTHY, WELL-GROWN, WELL-WATERED, AND WELL-FED PLANTS THAT WERE PLANTED ON TIME EARLY IN THE SEASON IS THE BEST CONTROL OF ALL. IF THAT'S DONE, THEY WILL RAPIDLY GROW OUT OF A LITTLE EARLY BUG DAMAGE. ALL OF THESE ORGANIC PRACTICES THAT KEEP AWAY DISEASE AND BUGS, IN ADDITION TO CROP ROTATION AND SANITARY GROWING HABITS, WILL PREVENT BAD THINGS FROM HAPPENING TO YOUR TOBACCO.

An Ounce of Prevention

While there are many diseases and pests that can affect tobacco in a home garden situation, you can pick off a few worms and avoid most of the main problems by following these tips and by being a good grower to begin with.

- Remove any possibly diseased or sick plants from the garden.
- Do not add infected plants to your compost; I recommend that you burn or place any diseased plants in the trash bin.
- Sanitation is critical. Keep your tools clean and sharp; you can clean your tools with a mild bleach solution.
- Wash your hands with a good antiseptic soap before you transplant or handle plants.
- If you smoke or chew tobacco, do not do so in the field and wash your hands before handling the plants. Experts debate whether TMV (tobacco mosaic virus) can survive modern processing but you may want to take this precaution.
- Provide good airflow around the plants by avoiding overplanting; overplanting is when you space the plants too closely together or near thick vegetation or other plants in the garden.
- Plant early—as soon as the frost-free date passes.
- Provide complete nutrition.
- Plant in an area that has good drainage, which means that

water flows though the soil and does not stand after watering or even after heavy rains. Standing water is your enemy.

- Keep the weeds out, both in the field between the plants and on the perimeter.
- Don't let the worms eat the tobacco leaves. When you see the worms, remove them. If the worms eat the plants, remove the eaten parts.
- Wash your hands *before* and *after* you visit the field. This should become a habit. Many commercial growers now require their workers to wear surgical type gloves before working with tobacco plants. This is a good idea, as you will find out after your first harvest, when you have sticky tobacco goo all over your hands.

Tobacco Mosaic Virus

Tobacco mosaic virus (TMV) is one of the more prevalent reasons why tobacco plants will die; it's spread by thrips primarily. TMV is a virus that is transmitted in the "veins" of tobacco plants, eventually weakening and killing them. It is spread from diseased tissue and it's also a disease that affects tomatoes and peppers. I mentioned in the garden preparation section in Chapter 4 that one of the first measures you can take against this disease is never to plant tobacco in the same location as you grew tomatoes or peppers the preceding year. This is why you must rotate your crops. You also should not continually plant tobacco in the same area every year.

There is no treatment, organic or not, that is truly effective. Good sanitation and growing practices are the keys to controlling this disease.

Blue Mold

Blue mold is just like it sounds—a blue-colored mold. It occurs when the plants stay too wet and there is poor airflow among them. It starts in the middle underneath the wettest areas. Prevention is accomplished by avoiding watering late in the day and picking off lower leaves early in the growing process to allow better air movement around the plants. Blue mold spreads quickly so, if you can, change the growing conditions if the plants are staying too wet, and destroy any affected leaves as soon as you see them by burning them or throwing them away.

Aphids

These small green-bodied insects poke holes in plant stems and leaves. Aphids like soft new plant growth. They are about a ⅛-inch diameter, can multiply quickly, and can seriously damage your plants. They can be controlled in several ways. Aphids can be simply washed off with a strong stream of water. They are also a favorite food of ladybugs. You can also spray a soap solution with a squirt bottle to control them;

Organic All-Purpose Bug Spray

You can make an all-purpose spray with one capful of liquid soap, a clove of minced garlic, a few blades of dried lemongrass, and a chopped jalapeño. Mix the garlic, lemongrass, and jalapeño in a gallon of water, boil it for 15 to 20 minutes, and strain the water. Set it aside and let it cool. Then add a capful of liquid Joy soap to the water.

This mixture will usually run off flea beetles and spider mites as well as aphids. Make sure the spray gets to the undersides of the leaves but note you can only kill bugs that are actually on the leaves at the time you spray. Spray only early in the morning before it gets hot so you will not burn the leaves. For the spray to work, you need to apply it two days in a row in order to kill the adult aphids and the nymphs (the next stage of their life cycle). Then wait a few days too see if you have done any good. A good example would be to spray them on a Saturday and Sunday morning and scout them again on Wednesday to see if they came back.

★ ★ ★ ★ ★ ★ ★ ★ ★ ★ ★

Aphids

the ratio is a capful of liquid Joy™ or horticultural soap (available at most garden centers) per one gallon of water. You can also use my recipe for an organic all-purpose soap bug spray.

Lacewings

Lacewings are soft-bodied insects that are approximately the size of a fly. They look just like the name implies and will be found on the undersides of leaves. All soft-bodied insects can be controlled by spraying the undersides of the leaves with the soap mixture I described for aphids.

Blue lacewing

Whiteflies

Whiteflies are a major pest of farm crops. When farmers spray their field whiteflies are driven up into the air in large swarms and rain down on the surrounding areas, even miles and miles away. They are now pretty resistant to even strong chemical pesticides. The main thing you poison with Sevin® dust is you and your family, so please do not use that. But whiteflies are soft-bodied insects and my soap spray works on them on contact. Remember, these bugs like to feed on the soft undersides of the leaves so this is where you will have to spray to kill them on contact. I had swarms in my garden the season I wrote this book, but they only fed on the oldest leaves that I should have already picked and thrown away anyway.

Flea Beetles

Flea beetles are small, black hard-bodied insects. They, like so many pests, usually attack the weeds and tall grass and will live there first. My all-purpose bug spray will work at running them off, but it may not kill them. Putting cheesecloth over seedlings and young plants will create a physical barrier that can help control them another way. The cheesecloth is typically placed over the plants a few feet above them. It can be placed directly

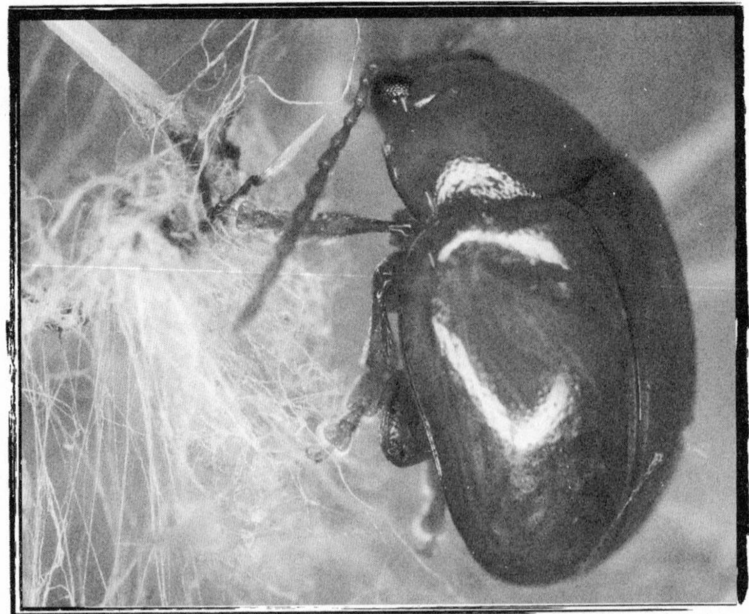

Flea beetle

on the plants but most gardeners build a support over the plants and lay the shade cloth on that. A support can be made from clotheslines and posts or even a wooden framework.

Spider Mites

Spider mites are not a common tobacco pest but sometimes they will attack tobacco. They usually attack plants that are under a great deal of stress. Spider mites are so small you need a magnifying glass to see them. They live on the undersides of the leaves, and give a leaf a pale, sickly appearance by poking tiny holes in the leaves. Spider mites attack the oldest and least healthy leaves first. There are several different types of mites, and some types are actually beneficial. The way to check for them is to rub the underside of the leaf with a white piece of paper. If there are small blood-colored streaks, then it is the two-spotted or red spider mites; they can ruin plants. If there are mostly black streaks, then those are the beneficial or good mites that just ate the spider mites for lunch. If you have two-spotted or red spider mites, remove the worst of the affected leaves and spray a 2 percent solution of horticultural oil (available online or in most retail garden centers) two days in a row to kill the adults and the eggs. This also works on many ornamental plants as well as tobacco. You should always follow the directions that are on the label. They are clearly written. Spray early in the morning only to avoid burning the leaves.

The spray must be dry before the bright sun hits the plants or you will have leaf burn.

Cutworms, Caterpillars, Budworms & Hornworms

The major caterpillar pests of tobacco are the tobacco budworm and the hornworms. Budworms will appear in the buds, as their name implies. Hornworms are mostly leaf feeders and will be easily recognized. Don't be dismayed if you find some leaves are chewed; tobacco has an amazing ability to compensate for lost leaf areas. You can pick them off by hand if you see them.

Cutworms and caterpillars will eat the older, thinner leaves. Pick the leaves or pick the caterpillars off. If they get ahead of you there is an organic solution. I must stress that keeping the weeds pulled and the grass short are the best preventions

Cutworm

Hornworm

because weedy beds and tall grass are where the cutworms are coming from. Bt (*Bacillus thuringiensis*) is an effective organic control that is readily available at retail garden centers. It usually comes in a dust but there are some spray forms. It takes a few days to work and affects the digestive systems of caterpillars and cutworms. I like to pick them off and drop them in the dregs of a can of beer, where they die a quick but happy death.

Healthy Plants and a Clean Garden Are the Ultimate Weapons

Remember: The best prevention is your own footsteps. You can often tell why a grower has problems before you even walk up to the field, because they aren't following these tips:

- Keep the area clean, neat, and organized.
- Healthy vigorous growing plants will have fewer problems.
- Cut the grass and pull the weeds.
- Keep your tools clean and sharp.
- Have a hoe and use it.

I know I am repeating myself on some of these things and you will hear it throughout the book. Take the time to enjoy your garden. It can be a pleasurable experience if you simply go out there every day, even if it is just for a few minutes. You will always find a few things that can easily be done that will improve your crop. Give your garden the time and attention it needs to ensure it is the best it can be. The best prevention of disease or pests is to maintain the habits I keep talking about. If you start having problems, try to identify why your plants are stressed. Stress can be caused by plants that are hungry, too wet, too dry, or neglected. Just like people, stress in plants is the cause of many of these problems.

If you feel you need to "kill some bugs" remember to spray the undersides of the leaves. The bugs attack the lowest, oldest leaves first. You can use the horticultural soaps and oils, such as Safer Soap® that is sold at retail garden centers, with great success. Spray in the morning and follow the guides on the label. I have also provided recipes for some homemade sprays that work as well; the one with the garlic, hot peppers, and lemongrass listed under aphid control will work as a preventative

in addition to being a contact bug killer. The only time you need to use the oil sprays versus the soap sprays is for spider mites (and spider mites will only attack very stressed out tobacco). They are more likely to be on other plants in your landscape and garden that are also stressed or old.

Harvesting Tip

Once you get close to harvesting, you should not be spraying or fertilizing.

HARVESTING, DRYING, AND CURING TOBACCO

6

ONCE YOU BEGIN TO HARVEST THE LEAVES AS THEY MATURE, YOU SHOULD PLAN ON HARVESTING TWO TO FOUR LEAVES PER PLANT, PER WEEK, FOR FIVE TO SEVEN WEEKS. THE QUALITY OF YOUR FINISHED TOBACCO PRODUCT WILL OFTEN BE DETERMINED BY THE QUALITY OF THE LEAVES THEMSELVES, THE TIMING OF THE HARVEST, AND THE LOCATION ON THE PLANT OF THE LEAVES YOU HARVEST.

You can expect to harvest mature, ripe tobacco leaves between 60 to 90 days after the seed was initially sown. The first bottom two or three leaves sometimes are referred to as "sand lugs" because they typically have sand and soil on them that is splashed up from the ground. Wash and dry them and this will be your first taste of the crop. They are not as high in nicotine but they are still better than commercially grown tobacco. Removing these bottom sand lugs is referred to as "priming" in the United States. These primer leaves need to be removed early in the growing process (a few weeks after transplanting)

You will need to pinch out any flower heads as they form unless you plan to save a few for seed. Pinching out, or "topping," is important. It removes a tobacco plant's apical dominance (the tendency to have a central stalk) and diverts energy, which will cause a plant to make suckers. These suckers rob vital nutrients from a plant and do not produce any usable leaves. Suckers should be removed by the home grower of tobacco by hand. Topping and removing suckers is important for all types of tobacco. Topping the flower heads sends a plant's vital energy to the remaining leaves to create the superior quality you desire.

Harvest No Leaf Before Its Time

It is important that you learn to recognize what a leaf looks and feels like when it is ready to be picked. The terms for the final stages the tobacco leaves go through on the plant are

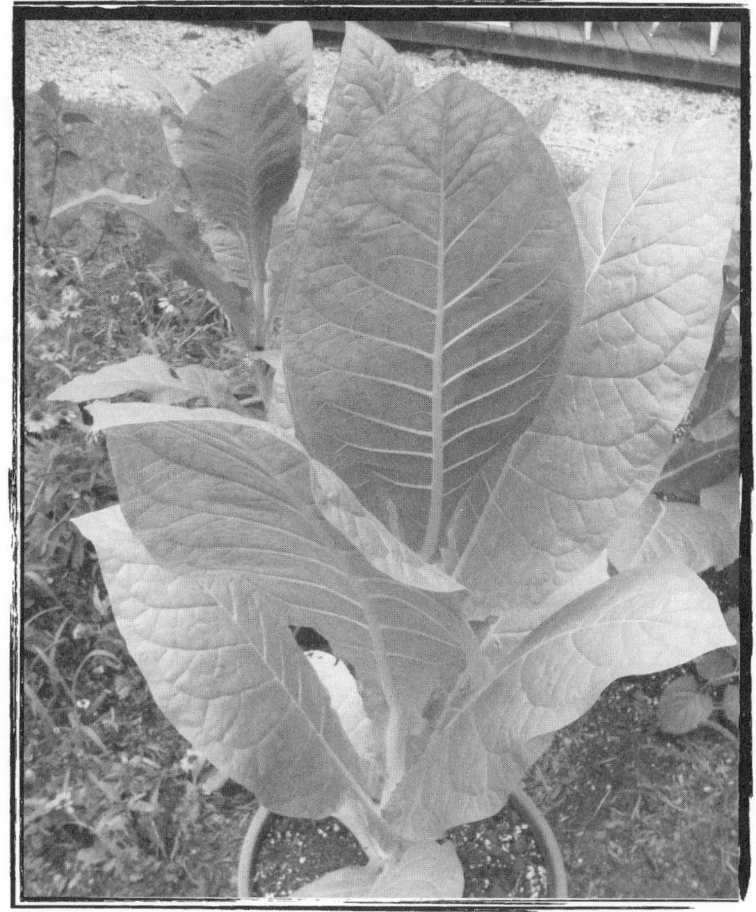

mature, ripe, and overripe. The identification of leaves that are ready to pick is considered an art form and pickers take great pride when it is time for them to make these decisions. Tobacco harvested at the perfect stage will produce the finest leaf in color, drying characteristics, quality, and weight. Overripe tobacco does not turn as good of a color and does not hold up to curing as well. (Note: burley, dark, and Perique types should be harvested by the whole plant, about 2 to 3 weeks after topping. The best quality and curing will be when the plant has been staked, hung, and cured. For these types, harvesting by leaf position compromises the overall quality. Once the leaves are cured, they should be separated from the stalk—this is called "stripping" tobacco. Generally, four separate stalks will yield a good mix for blending your final tobacco product.)

Leaves will be at the mature stage a few days before they are considered ripe. The first sign is a slight yellowing and puckering between the veins. The best quality is achieved when they are allowed to proceed to the ripe stage, which I can best describe as having an even golden glow about them. Overripe happens a few days later when the edges begin to show burning or browning. It is important to harvest leaves that are consistently at the same stage with each group. This allows you to focus on them as a group in the curing process. The lower leaves, which are the ones called primers, are the lowest quality and the upper leaves are the highest quality. It's the upper leaves that will have a higher percentage of the quality of grade that will be suitable for cigar wrappers. In Cuba, they try to overcome some of the quality differences in the leaves from their position on the stalk by placing the leaves picked lower on the stalk in the lower sections of their giant drying barns and placing the thicker upper leaves in the tops of the barns where it is warmer. Cigar makers, in particular, are very picky about when each section of leaves is harvested to ensure that each level will cure and dry at the same

rate. Cigarettes, pipe and chewing tobacco, and less expensive machine-rolled cigars tend to be blends of all of the different grades of leaves so there is a little more leeway. Manufacturers of high-quality boutique hand-rolled cigars are the pickiest and have the highest quality control standards throughout the harvesting and curing process.

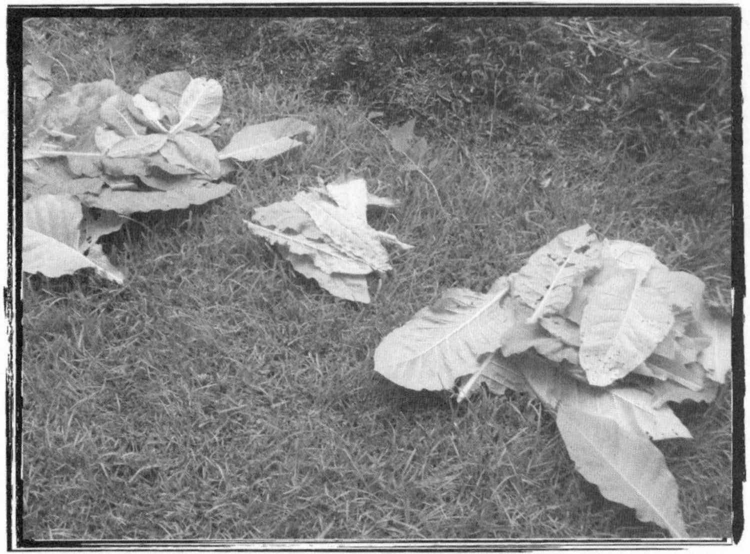

When the leaves are ready, harvest from the bottom up as the leaves ripen. Harvesting is typically done in the morning after the dew has dried and in the evening after the sun has abated a bit. The last stage of harvesting usually involves threading a spike or string through the stem, which can be tied to a stick or tying them in bundles with twine (these are called "hands" and typically are in groups of 25 for cigar making). Because you're only growing a few tobacco plants, you can tie them together neatly by the stems in pairs. This part is a personal preference and is determined by how you will be hanging them and drying them. Some growers will let leaves wilt a bit in the field and shrink some but the idea is to prepare them for drying and handling. It is common in some areas to harvest the entire plant at once after the first few pickings.

Drying and Curing

The process of drying and curing tobacco can be done many different ways based on how much time you have, how much tobacco you have, what your goals are for the end product, and your location. One important distinction is that good tobacco is not dried as much as it's cured, and it happens simultaneously.

I will review several different methods but I first want to explain the basic goals of what you are trying to accomplish and the stages that you must go through to have a usable product. Drying and curing, just like growing and harvesting, has been considered an art form throughout the years. It can be done very quickly as in flue-cured and sun-cured tobacco. It can be a very slow process in a barn or air cured. Smoke can be used to color and finish the tobacco as well as control the temperature and humidity. Depending on its type, tobacco can be flue-cured (Virginia) with heat; dark-fired with smoke; or air-cured (burley, dark air, and Oriental).

It can be dried in your house or outside in your garage. You can make a tent with plastic sides and hang that over a portable heater with a wet pair of jeans draped over it to control moisture and dry leaves on a clothesline. If you are really in a hurry, you can wash the sand lugs and dry and cure them in the microwave; the taste is kind of harsh but not completely bad. You will need to decide which method fits you, your goals, and your tastes.

Color and Chemical Changes

No matter what your preferred method ends up being, the reason to do this process is to get the color where you want it and start the chemical changes needed to make the leaves palatable. Of course, if you harvest the leaf at the perfect stage of yellow all you need to do is hang it up in a dry place for a few weeks until it is completely dry. Make sure there is plenty of ventilation and air movement. You also want to make sure the leaves are hung so that they are not touching one another. A closet containing a hot water heater is a good location; inside an air-conditioned or heated house will suffice. You can also build your own mini barn to flue-cure tobacco or build your own smoking barn (which can also be used to smoke meats).

Just as I said for your seedlings and for your garden, the best advice I can give you regarding tending to tobacco drying is to keep a close eye on it. If the place you have placed it to cure is nearby, be it the barn or in your kitchen, you will see if it is getting too dry or if it is drying too slowly. Commercial farmers constantly check on their barns. If they hit a long, rainy, cool spell then the doors will be shut and they will build a small fire to drive out any moisture. If you have the leaves hanging in a closet with your hot water heater and they are still staying too wet, run a fan on them or get some air moving before the leaves start to mildew. The ways to really ruin a tobacco harvest are to pick green leaves and dry them so

fast that they stay green even when they're dried, or to let them stay wet with no air movement for so long that they mildew. If the leaves mildew, you should throw that batch away. You should be harvesting in cycles, so you will have time to play around and manipulate the conditions until you find the drying process that best suits your situation.

Three Stages of the Drying Process

1 The initial color change needs to be to yellow, a process called, of course, "yellowing." Color determines 75 percent of the market value in commercial production. This initial yellowing occurs when the starch in the leaves is converted to sugar. In flue-cured drying the process starts slowly to allow this chemical change to fully take place and bring the whole barn to yellow. This is during the first 24 to 36 hours and only gentle heat is applied with temperatures in the 90 degrees F range and humidity between 85 to 90 percent. Remember, if you harvest perfect leaves they will already naturally be yellow. This yellowing process is finalized by basically keeping the leaves alive for the first day or so. At the end of this stage the leaves should be a bright yellow consistently throughout. If they do not turn yellow but remain green, you have harvested too early.

2 The next stage is actually the drying stage. What you want is to stop the chemical process and drive out

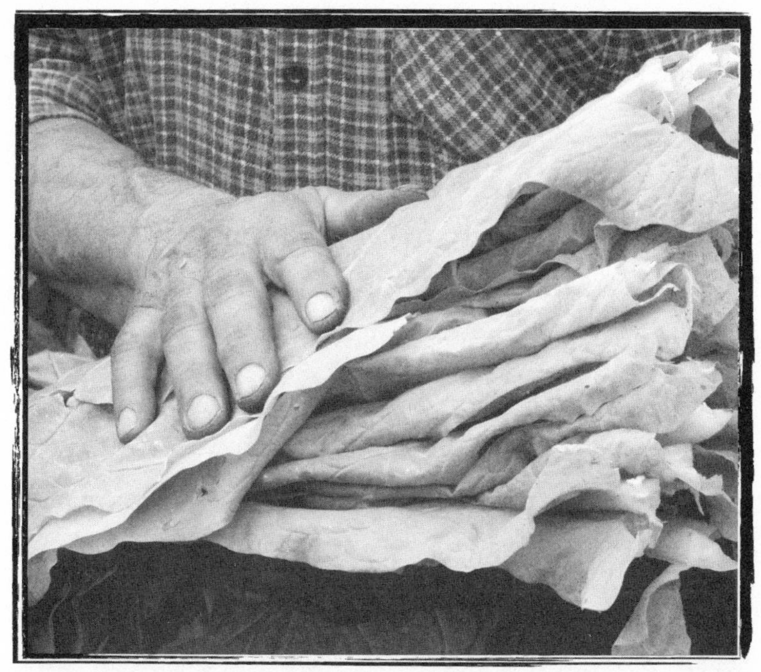

the moisture. If you wait too long to start drying and applying heat this will cause a dark brown vein to appear. If you apply too much too fast then you will get a dark discoloration of the leaf called scalding. In situations where you can apply heat, raise the temperature 4 to 6 degrees per hour until it reaches 170 to 180 degrees F. Maintain this temperature for 18 to 24 hours for complete drying all the way to the midrib. You could use your smoker for this. This is the stage in which the fires historically were (and still are) lit in the fire-cured barns. I just hung my tobacco leaves in my office with the air conditioner running and, because it was summer, they dried in two to three weeks. Flue-curing produces the bright yellow tobacco for high-end cigarette flake. In Cuba, they hang them in the barns on sticks and the process takes four or five weeks; they end up turning a darker color.

3 The next phase is called "ordering" or bringing the tobacco "in order." It is basically allowing moisture to return to the leaves (rehydrate) so that you can handle them. When tobacco leaves are extremely dry, they are very brittle and will crumble. Ordering can be done with high-pressure mist nozzles in a flue-cured chamber. In barns, it is done by opening the doors in humid climates and letting the outside air do the job. I saw an online video clip of a guy who lived in an arid area who made a tent and put wet jeans over a heater. You can mist the leaves with a hand sprayer; just be sure to use distilled

water and hang them back up afterwards. In general, the idea is to make the tobacco flexible enough to handle without breaking it to pieces. This process should not take longer than overnight, and it can be accomplished in a few minutes. Once they are flexible, you are ready for the next stage. Do not let them sit around moist without going to the next stage quickly or they will begin to mildew.

Curing

The goal of curing is to age the tobacco and force the respiration or fermentation of the sugars you just converted. This can be done in several ways and over varying time frames, each developing different levels of flavor.

The easiest thing to do is just hang the leaves in the rafters of a shop, barn, or garage in humid climates. You can just pull some leaves down when you want a smoke or chew. Tobacco will take several months or even up to a year to reach its peak flavor, but it is useable after 5 or 6 weeks. You can grab a bundle of it and cut it with a sharp knife after removing the stems and midrib to make cigars or cigarettes. You can also use a grinder (I used an antique sausage grinder), and grind it up to make fine-cut tobacco. You can blend the drier, bright tobacco with some of the wetter, darker tobacco to make cigarettes. You can grind up the darker stuff to make pipe tobacco. This is what I did, and I was very happy with the results. I left some in the low humidity environment and mixed it with the crop hung on my screened-in porch. This blend used in cigarettes burned nicely. You can also make up your own special blends after grinding a tobacco leaf and then storing the ground leaf in a jar to hold the right amount of moisture. If it dries out too much, add an orange peel and seal the jar to add a little moisture until it's back to the correct level.

Dampen the tobacco with a hand-held mister using distilled water and then form it into a block with a homemade or store-bought press. Be sure to remove the stems and midrib. The press can be constructed by making a small wooden box, 3 inches by 6 inches by 4 inches tall, out of ¾-inch plywood fastened with screws. Cut a piece of wood that fits inside the box like a lid. Place a nice leaf inside as a liner and then pack it with the moistened tobacco. Place two heavy-duty C clamps over the lid and under the bottom and tighten them down until the tobacco is pressed into a tight plug. This process will squeeze out a good bit of juice. Take this block and wrap it tightly in several layers of aluminum foil; then bake it in the oven at 175 degrees F or lower for 12 hours to cure it. This block can be shredded with a tobacco-shredding machine, or in a meat grinder attachment, or even in a food processor. You can also bite off chunks and chew it. It can be stored shredded in a sealed jar to be used for cigarette or pipe tobacco. This will be similar to what is known as fine-cut tobacco. You can add a little rum or whisky to it at this stage. It can be smoked right away, but the flavor will

mellow over time. The plugs will also keep well and mellow over time if they've been pressed, as well. There is a good video on YouTube showing a guy doing this.

You can boil tobacco in rum and water or other flavorings, adding a little sugar, and then press and shred it and store it as a

plug. This removes a little more nicotine and produces a milder flavor more quickly, although it will still improve with age. This is typically how Cavendish style pipe tobacco is cured.

You can ferment tobacco like the cigar makers do if you have enough volume to make a stack thick enough to build up heat in the center. Just like composting, a similar process, this method is very labor intensive, but it's another way to go about it. The internal temperature of the pile needs to reach 180 degrees F. After a few days, it needs to be restacked and flipped over to go through another heating cycle. This will need to be repeated until all of the pile is cured and it no longer heats up or ferments when it's turned. This is made easier in Cuba and other areas in the Caribbean by tying leaves in bundles of 25 leaves called "hands." Loose moisture is shaken off of the leaves with each turn. A thermometer is pushed in a pipe stuck through the center of the pile to monitor the temperatures. Workers constantly spray the pile with water during the process. They get the moisture just where they want it by taking the stack apart, shaking out any loose moisture, and allowing the hands to dry a bit for a few days (but still remaining flexible). You basically keep re-stacking it until it will no longer build up heat inside. They then press them into bales and store them.

You can also press tobacco leaves into large bales of any size and wrap them in burlap. You will want to use plywood and boards and use heavy ratchet straps or ropes to apply pressure. Be careful that the leaves in the bale are just moist with humidity and not too wet or it will mildew. A bale will store for a long time like this.

Tobacco keeps very well when it's stored in a dry, dark place and, like wine, it improves with age. Some tobacco used in manufactured cigarettes may be up to 10 years old. By carefully drying and storing tobacco, you can support your tobacco habit for several years. Store your tobacco in tins or jars in a dark place. Some people prefer to use a humidor of some type to store cigars or loose tobacco. A humidor is basically a box or chamber that allows you to control the moisture level surrounding the tobacco.

Whether you have grown a few pounds to last a season or if you have grown enough to last for years, your smoking preferences will determine the methods you choose to store your tobacco. The bottom line is, after drying, tobacco needs to be stored in an area that allows you to maintain enough moisture that it will be preserved, but not so much moisture that it will mildew. A carport or garage or even an attic (if you hang the tobacco) will work in areas that have humidity through the winter. In drier climates, you will need to compress blocks or bales for large amounts or rely on sealed containers (such as jars) to maintain the moisture content. Of course, you can always leave it to ferment under pressure in a barrel like the Cajuns do for the Perique tobacco. Zip-lock bags will work but you may have to occasionally add a little moisture by inserting a damp (not dripping) paper towel.

APPENDIX

ROLLING YOUR OWN CIGARETTES AND CIGARS

WHILE TRAVELING IN EUROPE IT IS HARD NOT TO NOTICE THE HIGH PERCENTAGE OF PEOPLE WHO STILL PREFER TO ROLL THEIR OWN CIGARETTES. WHILE IT IS MORE ACCEPTABLE THERE THAN IN THE UNITED STATES, YOU WILL GET SOME LOOKS FROM PEOPLE WHO ARE SHOCKED BY SEEING SOMEONE WALKING AROUND SMOKING WHAT APPEARS TO BE MARIJUANA. YOU MAY WANT TO ROLL YOUR CIGARETTES A LITTLE BIT FATTER AND PLACE A FILTER IN THEM SO THAT THEY LOOK MORE LIKE A CIGARETTE.

Hand-rolling your own cigarettes takes some practice. Using a rolling machine makes it easier to roll cigarettes. There are simple machines that have two rollers and there are some fancy machines that push out a very neat, perfect tube with the filter inserted.

There are differing opinions on how to start the rolling process. Some people prefer to take the rolling paper and crimp the paper to turn up the ends so it looks like a boat. This keeps the tobacco from falling out as you roll it. Some people just pack the tobacco in it and let it fall back into the jar or bag as it's rolled. The idea is to place an equal amount of tobacco down the length of the paper, and then roll it with both hands in a twisting motion between your thumbs and fingers. The trick is to get the leading edge of the paper to tuck in around the tobacco so when you finish it is tightly rolled. Some people like to place a dollar bill around the paper and tobacco to help tighten it as you roll. You will need to roll it often and back it off a bit and roll again to get it tight enough. You can place a small rectangle of rolled-up paper to act as a filter in the end, or you can buy actual filters and place them in the end. Don't forget to make sure that the glue edge of the paper is facing you on the top as you roll so you can lick it and stick it.

There are many different types of rolling papers. Some are made from rice and some are actually fine papers. In Holland, I noticed they prefer the longer papers and use rolled cardboard or cotton wad filters on one end. A homegrown, hand-rolled cigarette will burn more slowly and last longer than a store-bought "ready roll," as they are sometimes called.

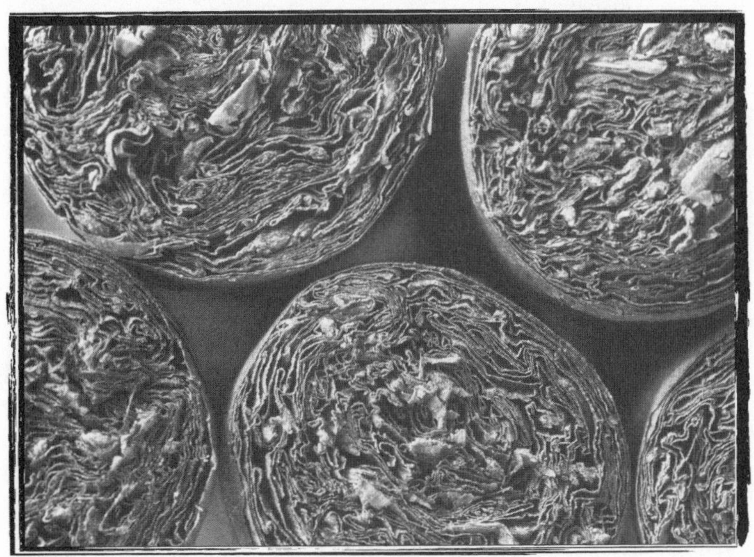

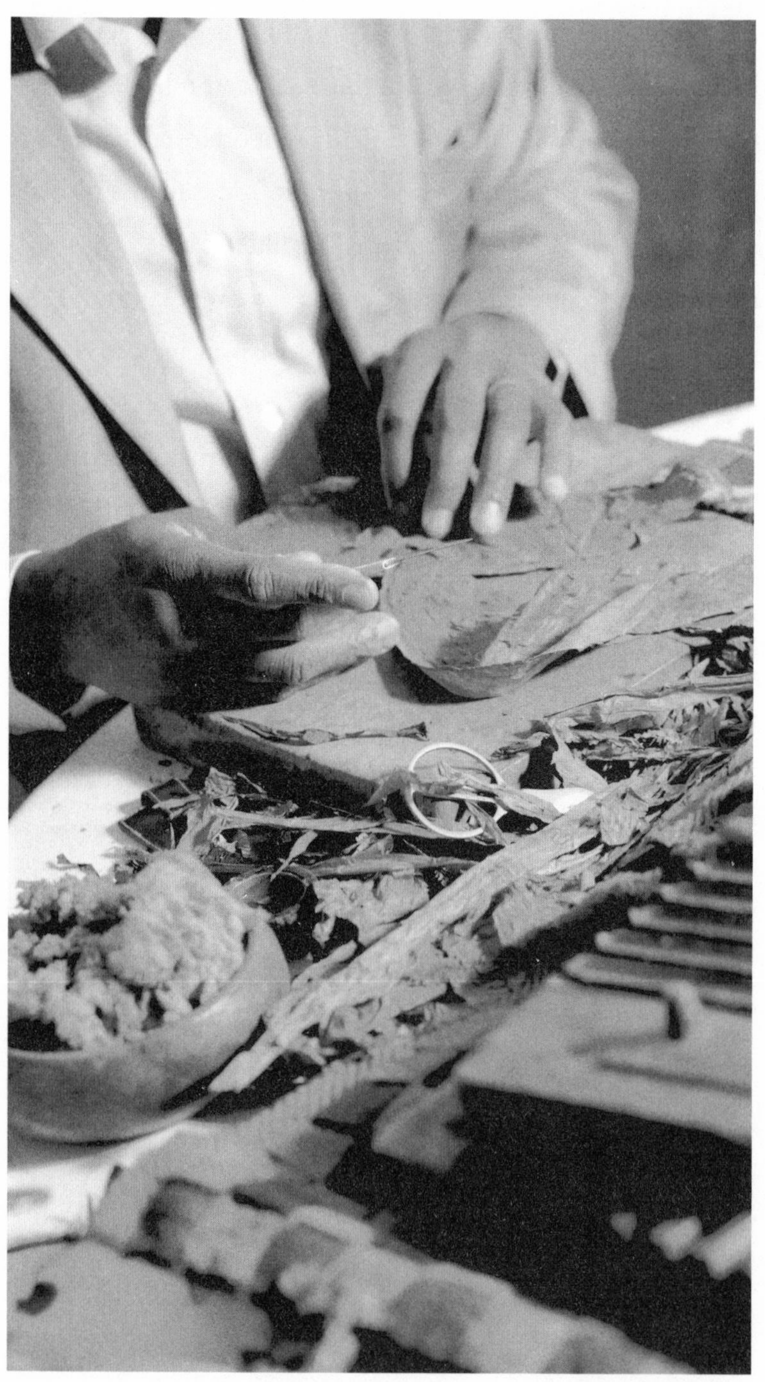

Rolling You Own Cigars

There are several good videos on the Internet showing how to roll a cigar. Just type in the phrase "roll your own cigar." Cigars come in many different sizes, shapes, and colors. They can be very long or short; they can be tapered on one end or both. The ring size refers to their diameter size. Although it takes years of practice for a cigar maker to achieve the status as a true master, a master cigar maker can produce a fine cigar in thirty seconds.

There are four main parts to a cigar: the cap, the filler, the binder, and the wrapper. The filler can be fine-cut or shredded. It can also be medium-sized pieces of tobacco. The filler is just what it sounds like—it fills the center. Finer cigars are made with select pieces for the filler and the cheaper ones are the fine-cut or slightly coarser tobacco. The binder is a large piece or two that runs the length of the cigar and holds the whole thing together as it is prepared for the wrapper. The wrapper is a perfect piece of a tobacco leaf that has no holes and is flexible enough to handle and roll. The wrapper pieces are preselected and usually kept in a special, tightly sealed tin can so they are kept a bit more moist and to keep them separate from the other

Tobacco Tidbit

It wasn't until the 1900s that the cigarette became the major tobacco product made and sold. Still, in 1901 3.5 billion cigarettes were sold, while 6 billion cigars were sold.

leaves. Filler tobacco sells for somewhere around 4 dollars a pound and cigar manufactures pay up to 40 dollars a pound for quality wrappers. The color and flavor of the wrapper often determine the grade and taste of a cigar. Caribbean, Central American, and Spanish cigar makers use a tool called a "chaveta" to cut the pieces for the wrapper, binder, and filler. This small, half-moon-shaped sharp knife with a handle on the straight side is also used to pack the cigar and roll it one last time under the flat side. There are many tools that can be used and which are more often seen in commercial applications. There are molds to hold the binder and wrapper under pressure until the master cigar maker puts it in a wrapper. Molds also determine and measure the ring size. You can find tools to cut and measure the length and there are automatic stem removers. A tool is often used to cut out the plug, which goes over the end of the cigar you smoke. The one product you will actually have to have besides a sharp knife and the tobacco is a sealer to hold the cigar together. A sticky substance called "pectin" is used by the professionals; pectin is the substance that binds the cells of fruit together. Pectin typically has no odor or taste. I used organic agave nectar and it works nicely as well.

Okay—now you are ready to make a cigar. First, select your wrapper based on the size and color cigar you would like. Then take the sharp knife or chaveta and cut the length of the leaf near its center vein. You can use either side of the leaf, left or right, but each side should be rolled from a different direction. Once the wrapper is ready, place the filler tobacco on top, add a longer binder leaf, and roll it up. Most people use a flat surface (such as a table) and roll the binder leaf diagonally around the filler, pressing down and rolling it several times to tighten it. You can pack them too tightly; if that happens, they will not burn very well. Once you wrap the binder around the filler, twist the ends and cut them to the desired length. The next step is to take your piece of wrapper and roll it diagonally with the outside of the leaf on the outside of the cigar. The best way to do this is to pull and tighten the wrapper from the bottom as you roll the cigar under your other hand. Then use a dab of sealer (I like agave nectar) on the leaf edge of the last wrap. Coat the tail end of the wrapper on both sides to make sure it sticks. This will be the side you smoke it from. Cut the cigar to the length you want. The last step is to cut out a small piece of leaf to make the cap. The cap is "glued" on the end of the cigar with the pectin or agave nectar.

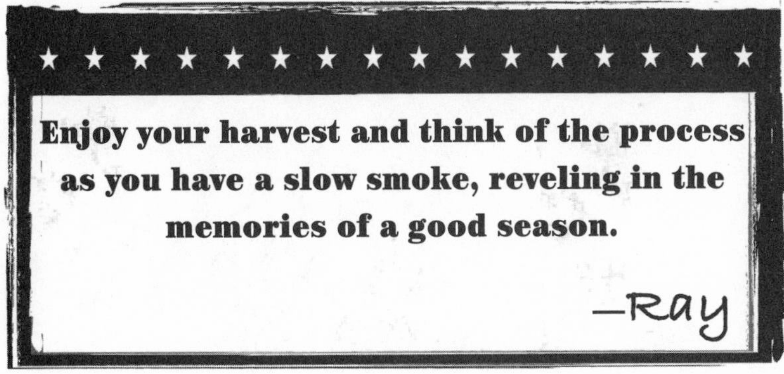

Enjoy your harvest and think of the process as you have a slow smoke, reveling in the memories of a good season.
—Ray

Sources

On page 30: Adapted from Gately, Iain. *Tobacco: A Cultural History of How an Exotic Plant Seduced Civilization*, 185–186. New York: Grove Press, 2001. Burns, Eric. *The Smoke of the Gods: A Social History of Tobacco*, 132. Philadelphia: Temple University Press, 2007. http://en.wikipedia.org/wiki/History_of_commercial_tobacco_in_the_United_States

On page 32: http://www.wramc.army.mil/Patients/diseases/wh/c7/pages/s5.aspx

On page 33: Adapted from Burns, Eric. *The Smoke of the Gods: A Social History of Tobacco*, 95 Philadelphia: Temple University Press, 2007. Burns, Eric. *The Smoke of the Gods: A Social History of Tobacco*, 95–96 Philadelphia: Temple University Press, 2007. http://en.wikipedia.org/wiki/History_of_commercial_tobacco_in_the_United_States

On page 36: Adapted from http://www.lib.ncsu.edu/exhibits/tobacco/thistory.html

On page 61: Adapted from 2009 report, Centers for Disease Control and Prevention. "Vital Signs: Current Cigarette Smoking Among Adults Aged ≥ 18 Years—United States, 2009." *Morbidity and Mortality Weekly Report* 2010;59(35):1135–40, accessed 2011 Mar 11. http://www.cdc.gov/tobacco/data_statistics/fact_sheets/fast_facts/index.htm

On page 149: http://academic.udayton.edu/health/syllabi/tobacco/history.htm

Bibiography and References

Print

Burns, Eric. *The Smoke of the Gods: A Social History of Tobacco.* Philadelphia: Temple University Press, 2006.

Collins, W. K., and S. N. Hawks, Jr. *Principles of Flue-Cured Tobacco Production.* Raleigh: NC State University, 1983.

Duggar, John F. *Agriculture for Southern Schools.* New York: Macmillan, 1923.

Gaitley, Ian. *Tobacco: A Cultural History of How an Exotic Plant Seduced Civilization.* London: Simon and Schuster, 2001.

Wiener, Jon. "Big Tobacco & the Historians." *The Nation,* March 15, 2010.

Web

Borio, Gene. "The Tobacco Timeline." Tobacco.org. Last modified November 20, 2010. http://www.tobacco.org/History/Tobacco_History.html

"Burley Tobacco Extension." University of Kentucky College of Agriculture. http://www.uky.edu/Ag/Tobacco/

"Dark Tobacco." University of Kentucky College of Agriculture. http://ces3.ca.uky.edu/darktobacco/

"Fertilizers, Soil Amendments, and Mulches." Common Ground. Accessed July 17, 2011. http://commongroundinpaloalto.org/fertilizers.htm

"Guide to Curing Tobacco." The Tobacco Seed Company. Accessed July 17, 2011. http://www.tobaccoseed.co.uk/Guide%20to%20Curing%20Tobacco.pdf

Killebrew, J. B., and Herbert Myrick. *Tobacco Leaf: Its Culture and Cure, Marketing and Manufacture.* New York: Orange Judd, 1910. http://www.archive.org/stream/tobaccoleafitsc00myrigoog#page/n8/mode/2up

Moore, J. Michael, and Paul E. Sumner. "Harvesting and Curing Flue-Cured Tobacco." University of Georgia College of Agricultural and Environmental Sciences. August 11, 2009. http://www.caes.uga.edu/publications/pubDetail.cfm?pk_id=6052

The Old Firm. "Tobacco Growing and Curing at Home." HubPages. Accessed July 17, 2011. http://hubpages.com/hub/Tobacco-Growing-and-Curing-at-Home

Organic Tobacco Production. http://www.attra.org/attra-pub/tobacco.html

"Tobacco." University of Georgia College of Agriculture and Environmental Sciences. http://www.caes.uga.edu/commodities/fieldcrops/tobacco/

"Tobacco Blue Mold." North American Plant Disease Forecast Center. North Carolina State University. http://www.ces.ncsu.edu/depts/pp/bluemold/

"Tobacco Curing." Ikisan. Accessed August 8, 2010. http://www.ikisan.com/Crop%20Specific/Eng/links/ap_tobaccoCuring.shtml

"Tobacco Growers Information Portal." NC State University.http://www.ncsu.edu/project/tobaccoportal/

Whittey, E. B. "Growing Tobacco in the Home Garden." EDIS. University of Florida Extension. February 2000. http://edis.ifas.ufl.edu/aa260

Resources for Seeds and Supplies

Common Ground—gardening supplies & education
www.commongroundinpaloalto.org
559 College Avenue
Palo Alto, CA 94306
(650) 493-6072

Heirloom Organics—seeds
www.heirloom-organics.com
3388 Merlin Road, Suite 400
Grants Pass, OR 97526
(877) 980-7222

Hime Harvest Garden Supply—gardening supplies
www.homeharvest.com
4870 Dawn Avenue
East Lansing, MI 48823
(517) 332-2663

New Hope Seed Company—seeds
www.newhopeseed.com
11208 Tidwell Rd, P.O. Box 443
Bon Aqua, TN 37025
(931) 670-5921

Seedman.com—seeds
www.seedman.com
1917 Summerlin Bayou Road
Vancleave, MS 39565
(no phone available)

The Tobacco Seed Company—seeds
www.thetobaccoseed.com
Online only

Thompson Cigar—cigar wrappers &humidors
www.thompsoncigar.com
5401 Hangar Court
Tampa, FL 33634
(800) 216-7107

Victory Heirloom Seed Company—seeds
www.victoryseeds.com
P.O. Box 192
Molalia, Oregon 97038
(503) 829-3126

Index

Growing My Own Tobacco

A Journal

The Tobacco Seeds I Started

Date:____

Type(s) of Tobacco: ____________________________

Notes:_______________________________________

____

____

____

____

____

The Tobacco Seedlings I Transplanted

Date:____

Note: ______________________________________

____

____

____

____

____

The Soil Amendments I Used

Date:____

Notes:_______________________________________

Where I Planted My Tobacco

Date:____

Notes:_______________________________________

How I Watered & Fertilized My Tobacco

Date:____

Notes:_______________________________________

How I Harvested & Cured My Tobacco

Date:____

Notes:_______________________________________

Meet Ray French

Ray French comes from a long line of large-scale farmers on both sides of his family, so his roots in the gardening and agricultural worlds run deep. French's great-uncle John Frederick Duggar started the Auburn University Old Rotation Farm Experiment in 1896. This test farm continues to be one of the most productive farms in Alabama, proving the value of crop rotations. Ray is committed to organic growing and is passionate about promoting sustainable agriculture—both of which he demonstrates in this, his first book.

Upon graduation from Auburn University with a degree in Nursery Crop Production, French ran some of the largest commercial growing operations in the country. Now, French is a consultant for a large home-improvement retailer. He travels the country and the world constantly, looking for great new plants to introduce to the American consumer. In fact, French can claim credit for playing an integral role in introducing one of the most popular plants in the United States today, the Knock Out® rose. In addition French helped introduce the Encore® Azalea and the SunPatiens® variety of sun-loving impatiens.

French lives in Fairhope, Alabama, with his wife and two sons, where he enjoys boating in addition to gardening for pleasure.